BOOK OF

CARS
AND
TRUCKS

POCKET

BOOK OF
CARS
AND
TRUCKS

SAM BROWN WITH ALAN BUNTING

KINGFISHER BOOKS

First published in 1987 by Kingfisher
Books Limited, Elsley House
24–30 Great Titchfield Street,
London W1P 7AD
A Grisewood & Dempsey Company

BRITISH LIBRARY CATALOGUING
IN PUBLICATION DATA
Brown, Sam
  Pocket book of cars and trucks.
  —(Kingfisher pocket books)
  1. Automobiles—Juvenile literature
  2. Trucks—Juvenile literature
  I. Title
  629.2'222   TL147

  ISBN 0-86272-271-3 Hbk
  ISBN 0-86272-270-5 Pbk

With thanks to Martin Lewis
Edited by Nicola Barber
Designed by Ben White
Illustrated by Michael Roffe
Cover design by Pinpoint Design Company
Phototypeset by Southern Positives and Negatives
(SPAN), Lingfield, Surrey

Contents

Introduction

For thousands of years people have relied upon their own muscles or those of animals such as oxen and horses to move them and their goods about. It is only over the last 100 years that all that has changed as the development of the car and the truck has gradually altered the face of the world. This book sets out to chart the history of this most important invention. Motorized transport has developed so fast that those automobile pioneers of the mid-19th century would not recognize today's sleek, fast cars and giant trucks as the successors to their own slow and spindly machines.

Today there are not many places left where the car is unknown. There are even a little two-seater on the Moon, although it is secondhand, having been left there after a successful Moon landing and expedition by one of the Apollo space missions. Although you won't find the Moon Buggy in the reference sections, and this book is not intended to be a complete spotters' guide, you will find descriptions and pictures of many of the cars and trucks you are likely to see being driven about, plus a few unusual and exotic vehicles that might not be so common.

Other sections of the book trace the progress of the car from the steam-driven vehicles of the 1800s to the present day, and examine some of the brilliant engineers who devoted a large part of their lives to helping the car to succeed through their clever solutions to so many of the problems that beset the early manufacturers.

The 100th birthday of the motor car has just been celebrated. If the rate of progress over that time is repeated over the next century, we are in for an exciting time!

◀ **Brooklands 9 March 1934.** The line-up for the first Walton Half Mile Scratch Sprint.

100 Years of Cars

During its comparatively short history of barely 100 years, the motor car has changed the face of the world and the lives of many of the people who live in it. The automobile has developed dramatically since the early days, just before the turn of the century, when pioneers such as Karl Benz were allowed to drive their new 'horseless carriages' in restricted areas only because it was feared that they might frighten both the horses and the people.

Today, it is the horse and carriage which is a rarity on the roads, and we take it for granted that we can easily cover 80 to 160 km (50 to 100 miles) in a couple of hours or so in a car. How different from the first real car journey made by Karl Benz's wife Berta in 1888 between the German towns of Mannheim and Pforzheim, which took many

▼ **Karl Benz's Motorwagen of 1885.** It was designed with a lightweight frame and wire-spoked, bicycle type wheels.

▲ **A Benz Viktoria** at the London
Motor Show of 1898. This model was
brought out in 1893, and was one of the
first cars to be produced in any number.

hours. Her spindly wheeled Benz tricycle could barely manage 6 km/h
(4mph) and Berta and her sons frequently had to get out and push it
up the hills. When it broke down, they mended it themselves and Mrs
Benz is said to have solved one problem by using her hat-pin. There
were no garages and, apart from having to make frequent stops at
houses to ask for water to top up the engine cooling system, Mrs Benz
turned a small pharmacy shop into the world's first filling station
when she asked the surprised chemist for a couple of litres of what we
now know as Benzine, to fill up her tank.

The arrival of the mobile steam engine in the form of the railway
train provided one of the most important developments leading to the
birth of the car. Whereas before many people never ventured beyond
their immediate neighbourhood, now trains allowed them to cover
long distances easily and quickly, and encouraged them to develop a
taste for travel. The problem was that they could only go where the
tracks went – what people really wanted was a form of independent
personal transport which did not rely on horses. The first obvious
answer was to try and combine old and new technology. This was

▲ **Thomas Rickett's steam carriage** was built for the Marquis of Stafford in 1858. Its top speed was over 19km/h (12mph). The man at the back, called the 'chauffeur', stoked the fire to keep it going.

attempted by taking a horse-drawn carriage and fitting a steam engine to it, but in many cases the results were not very satisfactory. Many potential pioneers gave up their new-fangled, smoking slow-coaches and returned to the old faithful horses which were quite often considerably faster.

Whose invention?

The question of who actually invented the motor car is disputed. Everyone thought that the answer would be found during the '100 Years of the Car' celebrations in 1986. These celebrations were to mark the centenary of the year in which Karl Benz submitted the patent for his 'Motorwagen', a three-wheeler powered by a single-cylinder gasoline type engine. But the French disagreed, saying that a M. Delamere-Deboutteville had produced a car some two years before. While there is some doubt about the authenticity of this claim, it is universally acknowledged that much of the pioneering work on the *powerplants* was carried out in France.

Benz's 'Motorwagen' and a number of other contenders of the time were all powered by internal combustion engines, operating on roughly the same principle as the engine used in the modern automobile. The alternative form of propulsion – steam power – has a much longer history. In China during the Chou dynasty of 1655 a Jesuit missionary is reported to have built a four-wheeled carriage powered by a steam turbine engine. Around 1770 a French army officer called Nicholas Cugnot produced a massive steam-powered tractor designed to replace horses as pullers of gun carriages. It was not a success. Its top speed was 5km/h (3mph) and thus considerably slower than a good team of horses. What is worse, Cugnot's steam wagon earned the title of the first 'car' to be involved in an accident when it went out of control and knocked down a wall. The army Generals were not impressed and ordered that its development should be stopped at once. More than 30 years later, the 'steamers' were still seeking recognition. In Britain, the famous steam engineer Richard Trevithick built and produced a steam carriage which worked well, but failed from lack of financial support. In America, Oliver Evans built an amazing device which he called the 'Snorting Swimmer'. It was in essence the world's first amphibious car being a steam powered undercarriage which he used to launch a dock cleaning pontoon.

But without doubt it is Karl Benz who is acknowledged as the 'father' of the motor car. He was working at the same time as another famous German engineer, Gottlieb Daimler, and although the two never actually worked together and it is claimed rarely, if ever, met,

▼ The first 'car' to have an accident. Cugnot's steam gun carriage of 1769 could travel at up to 5km/h (3mph).

their names are linked in the title of one of the most important car companies in the world. Daimler Benz, or as it is more popularly known, Mercedes-Benz, is one of the longer lasting companies. Others have been less lucky and only a handful of the 4500 makes of private car registered since 1896 are still around today.

▼ The car that brought motoring to the masses, a Ford Model T of 1915. The 'Tin Lizzie' was easy to maintain and cheap to run. It had a top speed of about 64km/h (40mph).

As with all strange and new inventions, the car suffered a great deal from public mistrust. Early motorists were strictly limited by controls such as the British 'Red Flag' Act of 1865. This Act required that every 'road locomotive' must be accompanied by at least three people – one to steer, one to attend to the fuel, and another to walk ahead with a red flag to warn people that the car was coming and also 'to help control restive horses'. The top speed allowed was 6km/h (4mph) in the country and 3km/h (2mph) in town. That law remained in force for 31 years. But the opposition to this new and exciting form of transport could not restrain its progress for long, and all around the world, the pace of development began to quicken. It was led initially by the French, with the rest of Europe and the USA not far behind. Public interest was stimulated by the growth of motor sport and in

◀ **Fernand Gabriel** won the last city-to-city classic, the 1903 Paris-Madrid race. His famous Mors is depicted here on the wall of the Art Nouveau Michelin Tyre building in London.

▶ **Marcel Renault** travelling at 129km/h (80mph) in the same race. This photograph was taken just before he was killed in one of the series of crashes which caused the French Government to stop the race at Bordeaux.

particular the epic long distance races such as the Gordon Bennett cup series, and the dashes between major cities such as Paris to Madrid, and even Paris to Peking.

However, the automobile was still a toy for the rich only; the real revolution which was to bring motoring to the masses had to wait until 1909. It was then that Henry Ford produced his Model T – the original 'Tin Lizzie'. This model lasted in production for almost 20 years and helped Ford to become the first car maker in the world to build and sell more than one million units in a year. It took the rest of the world more than 40 years to catch up with Ford, but Volkswagen hit the magic million in 1962 with another evergreen design – the VW Beetle.

Today, the number of cars and trucks on the roads of the world is staggering. Designs have advanced so dramatically that even a modest family saloon can be capable of exceeding 160km/h (100mph) using an engine only a fraction of the size of those used in the monster racers of the 1900s. It is not the basic principle of the machine which has changed but the methods and materials used to make it as they have followed human progress from riding horseback to market to

▲ **A car for the rich** and famous, a 'stretched' Lincoln.

riding a rocket to the Moon. Cars will now talk to you and tell you what is wrong. They have on-board computers to calculate how much fuel you have used, how long you have been travelling and what time you are likely to arrive at your destination. Devices which provide navigational directions, allow you to throw away your maps and still find your way. A sophisticated in-car entertainment system with radio, tape and compact disc player can be as powerful as many discotheque set-ups. Telephones and air-conditioning are becoming commonplace and some of the big limousines even have refrigerators and televisions. One American owner has created what must be the ultimate limousine by adding a few extra feet to the coachwork in order to accommodate a swimming pool and sauna cabin!

In recent times two main factors have affected the automobile and its development: the fuel crisis of the early 1970s prompted by the Arab/Israeli war, and the increasing awareness that exhaust gases from cars should be made cleaner to prevent further damage to the environment. In both cases, the response from the car makers has been positive, and their engineers have worked hard to make modern cars use less fuel and produce fewer harmful fumes – chiefly by modifying old engines, and designing new ones to run on petrol which does not contain any lead.

The Driving Force

The early cars demonstrated an attempt to combine the established skills of building horse-drawn coaches and the new and· exciting development of the steam engine. But while steam power worked for railway engines, where overall weight was no real concern and where regular stopping places to take on water and fuel could be easily provided, it was a different matter for the car. Carrying water and fuel meant less room for passengers and the cars had extremely limited range.

▼ **The French Scotte Steam Wagonette** was on the roads in the early 1890s. It took over 30 minutes to build up steam, and could carry two passengers at a top speed of about 12km/h (7mph).

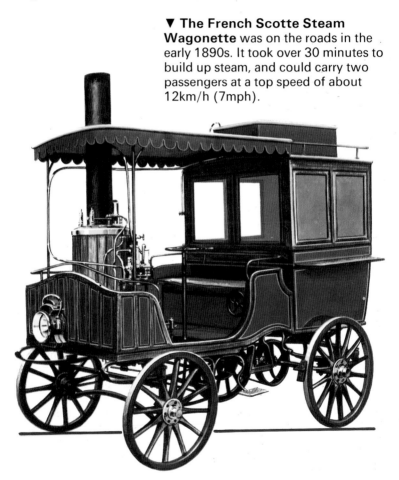

Most of the steam cars built were American – President William Taft used a White steam car for official functions. The New York Police Department bought a few White steamers in 1908 for use as prowl cars. Steamers have held the World Land Speed Record twice, the second time in 1906 when a Stanley Special reached 205km/h (127.5mph) at Ormonde Beach, California.

Electric cars are still considered to be the best answer to problems of noise and fume pollution. The most recent (but unsuccessful) attempt to market an electric car was by British computer tycoon Sir Clive Sinclair with his C5 runabout, proposed as the first of a series of revolutionary electric vehicles. Since the early days of the car, designers and engineers have been striving to develop motors and powerful lightweight batteries to replace the petrol engine, but without success. Between 1896 and 1939 some 565 different makes of electric car were registered but, like Sir Clive's enterprise, they were all very short-lived. It is interesting to note that the first road vehicle to exceed 96km/h (60mph) was electric powered: the torpedo-shaped single-seater called *La Jamais Contente* (Never Satisfied) achieved a

◀ **La Jamais Contente,** the record-breaking electric car. It had a powerful motor on the back axle and the smallest wheels of any car yet built.

▶ **Modern experiments with electric cars.** Sir Clive Sinclair in his C5.

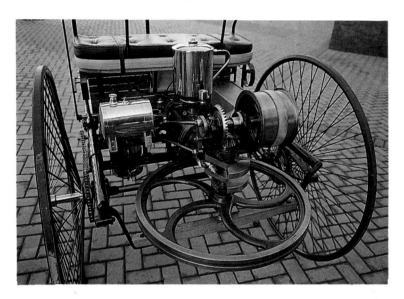

speed of 105.87km/h (65.79mph) in 1899. An electric car also took part in the Paris to Bordeaux race in 1897, but it needed fresh batteries every 26km (16 miles).

Meanwhile, Benz, Daimler and others were working to produce internal combustion engines, running on a mixture of petroleum spirit and air, which could be fitted into a carriage. The Benz tricycle was powered by a two-stroke single-cylinder engine of 1.7 litres. The huge piston and flywheel turned a pulley via a series of gears to drive a chain running from a shaft to a rear wheel. A long lever at the side of the footboard controlled a primitive form of clutch to disconnect the engine from the drive. The engine turned so slowly that you could hear every firing stroke, the vibration from which shook the little car on its fragile spoked wheels.

The 'Otto' cycle

The modern car engine is merely a more sophisticated version of that Benz motor. The principle is the same except that today's engines are much more efficient, smaller and certainly quieter. Almost all modern engines work on the four-stroke or 'Otto' cycle (named after the company of Otto and Langen for whom Gottlieb Daimler and Wilhelm Maybach worked while designing the first practical engine of this type). The 'Otto' cycle works by using a piston running inside a cylinder. On the first downward stroke the piston sucks in a mixture of fuel and air. It then pushes up, compressing the mixture which is ignited, causing it to explode and expand. The pressure of this expansion forces the piston down providing the power stroke of the sequence. On the next up stroke, the burned gas or exhaust is pushed out and the pattern begins again. The piston is linked to a shaft in the bottom of the engine which is turned by the action and from this the drive can be taken to the wheels of the vehicle by gears, belts or chains.

That first engine ran at about 800 revolutions per minute. Modern engines regularly run at 6000 rpm and racing engines up to double that speed. Small cars usually have four cylinders, although there are some with just two or three. Six cylinders in a line is common in bigger cars and the higher performance vehicles can have eight or 12 cylinders arranged in a vee, four or six each side.

There have been a number of attempts to get away from this basic four-stroke principle, but none has really proved to be a commercial success apart, perhaps, from the rotary engine patented by Felix Wankel in which the pistons are replaced by a triangular rotor. The motor is small and smooth running, but so far only the Japanese Mazda company has treated it seriously and used it for volume production in its RX-7 sports car.

▼ **The four-stroke** or 'Otto' cycle.

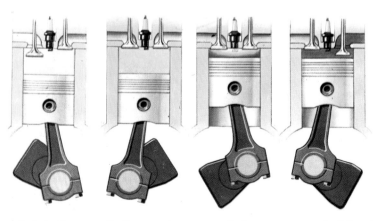

| 1. Induction | 2. Compression | 3. Power | 4. Exhaust |

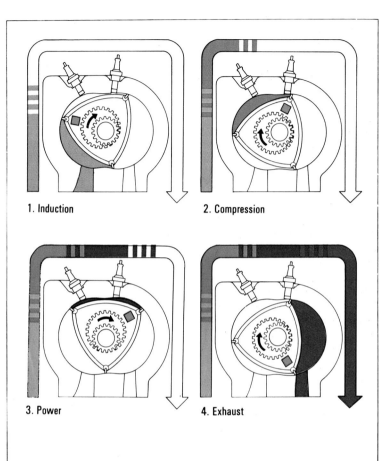

1. Induction

2. Compression

3. Power

4. Exhaust

THE WANKEL ROTARY ENGINE

The Wankel rotary engine is probably the most successful alternative to the more widely used piston engine as a power unit for cars, but the operating principle is very similar. Instead of using the piston to draw in and compress the air/fuel mixture, it uses a triangular rotor, operating inside a special chamber shaped like a flat figure of eight, but described by the engineers as epitrochoidal. The diagram shows the four phases of induction, compression, power and exhaust, like the four strokes of a conventional piston engine, except that with the rotary, that sequence happens three times for every complete revolution of the rotor. Because the range of movement of the mechanical parts is so limited, the engine is remarkably smooth and vibration-free.

▲ **The Mazda RX-7** is one of the few
cars in volume production to replace the
traditional pistons with the Wankel
rotary engine.

As for fuel – before the arrival of the motor car, petroleum spirit
was regarded almost as a waste product, but the rapid spread of the
automobile meant that oil and its refined products such as petrol were
in big demand. Only recently have people begun to accept the fact
that one day we might run out of oil and so the effort to find an
alternative fuel has continued, albeit in fits and starts. A wide range of
weird and wonderful alternatives has been considered and tried. They
include fuel from the peel of oranges and other fruits, and alcohol
made from potatoes. It is true that you can turn almost anything into
fuel, provided that cost does not matter, but so far oil fuel is the best
compromise, although Brazil has been successful in large scale
production of alcohol fuel from sugar cane, and in many parts of
Europe filling stations offer liquid natural gas to fuel suitably
converted cars.

Motor Sport

▼ **Truck racing** at Brands Hatch.

The motor car was not too many years old before people began to think of it as more than just a means of transport. They quickly discovered that cars could be fun and what more fun than racing your car against another to see which is fastest? – motor sport was born.

Today, motor sport covers many different areas with a collection of weird and wonderful specialist vehicles from tiny go-karts to huge racing trucks. There are races over deserts and swamps as well as the special race tracks for the sophisticated Formula One cars. In fact, if it has wheels, you can race it.

But sport does have a serious side effect: motor sport competition has been responsible for almost all the major advances in car design over the years. Whereas manufacturers would be reluctant to try something really new on a customer, they might risk it on a racing car. If it worked, the racing car could be used to develop it and iron out all the problems. Later it might be fitted to a production car for public sale. Another serious side to motor sport is advertising. Manufacturers with a successful racing or motor sport connection can use it to support the ordinary product, even though so many of today's sporting cars bear little or no relation to the vehicles you can buy.

23

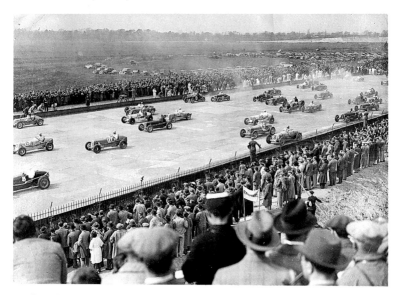

▲ **Racing at Brooklands in 1936.**
The JCC International Trophy Race.

The Beginnings

It wasn't always like that. In the early days of the car, there were some
great races between major cities in which the big companies of the day
such as Renault, Peugeot and Fiat used to battle it out. These races
were on ordinary roads, with little regard for the safety of the public,
the drivers or their unfortunate 'riding mechanics'. These mechanics
had a rough time, hanging on for grim death in crude unpadded seats,
seeing to the lubrication and fuel pumps, leaping out to mend
punctures and change wheels, and running the risk of being thrown
out at almost every bend. It was thrilling stuff, but highly dangerous –
the picture on page 15 shows Marcel Renault just before a fatal
accident in one of these races. The rising toll of deaths among
competitors and the public soon forced the motor sport organizers to
continue their racing on restricted tracks.

Road racing continued for many years and today there are still at
least two major race events that take place on public roads – the
famous 'round the houses' Grand Prix of Monaco, and the equally
famous Le Mans 24 hour endurance race. But these are not on open
roads. The Monaco circuit and the public road section of the Sarthe

▲ **Tony Brooks** in the Monaco Grand
Prix of 1957.

circuit at Le Mans are closed off for the duration of the race. It is not surprising really. Some of the fastest cars at Le Mans, for example, are capable of speeds over 321km/h (200mph). Once the race cars were restricted to proper circuits, there was less need for mechanics to ride with the driver. Now they could wait, with spare parts, tyres and fuel, by the track side in areas which are still called the 'pits'. Without the mechanic there was no need for two seats and so began the development of the single-seater racing car, and possibly the most glamorous form of motor sport.

Pressured by companies anxious to win races with their products, the racing car designers forced the pace of advance and the pace of the races. Speeds rose, requiring the team managers to seek corresponding improvements in the performance of suspension, steering and braking.

Europe remained the centre of motor sport, chiefly because all the major teams and the big circuits, such as the famous Brooklands banked track, were there. The Italians, including Alfa Romeo and Maserati tended to dominate the scene in the 1920s and 1930s, but the end of the '30s and the approach of the Second World War (1939–45) saw the emergence of the Germans, and in particular Mercedes-Benz and Auto Union, to take over the leadership. Post war, racing continued with some of the old names still there, but joined by newcomers such as Vanwall, Cooper and the British company, Lotus taking on the might of Ferrari and Maserati. A major change occurred when it was realized that in order to be competitive, teams had to start spending large amounts of money and the only way to get that money was by advertising and sponsorship. This led to today's slogan-festooned race cars, sponsored by a curious collection of companies making anything from clothes to yoghurt.

Racing Today

The modern race car is a triumph of technology, in many cases using materials and techniques borrowed from aerospace. Besides single-seaters, there are also sports/racing cars with all-enveloping, aero-

▲ **The Benetton-BMW racing car** that took part in the 1986 Grand Prix season, driven here by Gerhard Berger. Formula One cars can get through ten sets of tyres in one event, and use about 25 engines every season.

▲ **The victorious** Peugeot Talbot
team in the 1984 San Remo rally.

dynamic bodywork which are capable of incredibly high speeds. In
the old days you could buy a car that came very close in looks and
specification to a race winner, today this is not possible – because
these cars cost millions of pounds. Times have changed for the drivers
too. They used to drive in ordinary trousers, short-sleeved shirts and
light leather helmets. Now they wear special flameproof suits, and
spaceman type helmets with built-in radio intercoms, and an oxygen
supply that can be turned on in the case of a crash and fire.

One of the branches of motor sport that is probably closest to
production cars is rallying. This involves driving cars over rough
territory as quickly as possible, through twisty forest roads, often in
snow and ice. This demands great skill and concentration on the part
of the driver and co-driver who will be calling out the route directions.
Rallies take place all over the world, in the snow and ice of Sweden
and the mud of Africa, and a world championship win is highly prized
by the manufacturers. In recent times, the design of rally cars has
begun to move away from the standard cars from which they were
supposed to have been developed. A series of bad accidents involving
these cars led the organizers to revise the already complicated rules to
make things safer, and the cars in the top classes, slower.

▲ **An American dragster,** with thick
back tyres and narrow motor cycle-type
front wheels.

Motor sport also includes going fast in a straight line and it is here
that the Americans reign supreme. The USA is the home of drag
racing, the sport in which the objective is to cover a quarter mile from
a standing start in the fastest possible time. There are a number of
different classes, but the most spectacular is the big 'rails', so-called as
the name suggests because they consist of two chassis rails carrying an
engine and huge driving wheels at the back, and tiny lightweight
wheels at the front. The driver sits behind the engine and has to wear
an asbestos flameproof suit and helmet. The big fat tyres are run up
before the start making them sticky to provide lots of extra grip. At
the events, the cars go off the line in pairs, leaving great trails of
smoke and flame. The run ends when the drivers 'pop' special
parachutes to slow the cars down.

Recently there has been a rapid growth in what are called
endurance events, where specially prepared cars take part in what
could be called a 'super-rally'. The most famous is the Paris-Dakar
event run across the Sahara desert and tackled by cars, special trucks
and even motorcycles.

The Trailblazers

These are some of the people directly responsible for the development of the motor car from the beginning to the present day:

Karl Benz
In 1885 he built the world's first motor car in Mannheim and his wife Berta is credited with making the first 'motor tour'. At one point he ran the biggest car manufacturing company with dealerships all over the world. He disliked motor sport and said that a car trying to go faster than 59km/h (37mph) would "shake itself to pieces".

Gottlieb Daimler
Born the son of a baker, Daimler began his working life as a gunsmith before joining engine makers Otto and Langen. With Wilhelm Maybach he designed the first 'high speed' petrol motor, the ancestor to the modern car engine. The patents sold worldwide. He founded the Daimler car company of Germany.

Karl Benz

Gottlieb Daimler

André Citroën

André Citroën

A forward-thinking French car designer and manufacturer who was responsible for a large number of innovations and advances, including production of cars without a separate chassis, and the replacement of traditional spring suspensions with a system using fluid and compressed gas.

Henry Ford

The man who popularized motoring by developing the methods to make good, reliable cars quickly and cheaply. The mass production systems set up at Ford's factory in Michigan were the forerunners of modern high volume car assembly plants.

Henry Ford

William C. Durant

William C. Durant

A carriage maker from Michigan in the USA, he was responsible for the start of the growth of General Motors, now the largest car manufacturing company in the world. Famous makes bought by GM over the years include Buick, Oldsmobile, Cadillac and Pontiac. Durant almost bought out Henry Ford, but ran out of money.

Charles Rolls and Frederick Royce

Two of the most famous men in the history of motoring, they founded one of the most famous firms, Rolls-Royce Ltd, in 1906. Their Silver Ghost, designed by Royce, set new standards of refinement and reliability for cars.

Charles Rolls

Frederick Royce

Milestones

Some of the important cars that have appeared during a century of motoring history.

1885 type Benz

Karl Benz combined existing cycle and coachbuilding knowledge with the new development of the gas engine, to produce what is recognized as the world's first true motor car. A three-wheeler, the car was powered by a 1.7 litre single-cylinder, two-stroke engine, water-cooled and with spark ignition, the latter being advanced for the time. The carriage-style bench seat could take two adults. The single wheel at the front was steered directly by a lever, giving a half turn from lock to lock. Drive to the rear wheels was by belt and pulley and chain. Its top speed was around 6km/h (4mph).

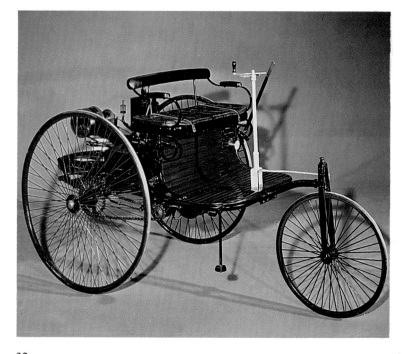

Ford Model T

The original 'Tin Lizzie', launched in 1909, was designed to fulfil Henry Ford's ambition to get the world on to four wheels. Although it was not technically advanced for the time, the Model T was tough and reliable. It broke all production records and was finally dropped from the Ford range after more than 15 million had been sold. Ford's clever mass production line did not allow for many variations in specification – including choice of colour – hence Ford's famous statement that Model T customers could have the car in any colour they liked, provided that it was black. The car had a 2.9 litre, four-cylinder engine which provided a maximum speed of 72km/h (45mph), and a fuel consumption of around 40km per gallon (25mpg). The brakes acted on two wheels only, and the Ford transmission system had just two forward speeds, but from 1920 buyers could order a Model T with an electric starter. It originally cost $850, but the cost was progessively reduced until, in 1925, it was possible to buy a Model T for as little as $260. Ford pioneered mass production methods, and opened a plant in Britain in 1911. In 1922 Model T production exceeded one million a year for the first time. It was replaced in 1927 by the Model A.

1911 Rolls-Royce Silver Ghost

Rolls-Royce Silver Ghost

The car that was to become known as the Silver Ghost first appeared at the London Motor Show of 1906, only two years after the first meeting between Frederick Royce and Charles Rolls. It was introduced as the Rolls-Royce 40/50 but was dubbed the Silver Ghost for two reasons. Firstly, because of the silver colour scheme chosen for the 13th car completed and secondly because of the fact that the 40/50, with its big six-cylinder, 7.0 litre engine was amazingly quiet compared with contemporary rivals – as silent as a ghost in fact. It was such a success that the company stopped making other models and concentrated solely on the 40/50, which remained in production until 1925 – one of the longest production runs in motoring history.

Duesenberg J

One of the great classic American cars produced on the instruction of Erret Cord, who had just bought the Duesenberg company, to build a dream car and not to worry how much it would cost. The Model J had a 6.9 litre straight-eight engine, producing 200 brake horsepower, making it the most powerful car on the road at the time. Later models had supercharging, giving them a potential top speed of 209km/h (130mph). Other modern features included servo-assisted hydraulic brakes and automatic chassis lubrication. You had to be rich to afford one. In 1928 the basic chassis cost $8500 and special coachwork double that price. Famous Model J owners included multi-millionaire Howard Hughes and film stars Gary Cooper and Clark Gable.

1934 supercharged Duesenberg SJ

Citroën *Traction Avant*

Generally referred to as 'The Traction', the Citroën Type 7 blazed so many new trails in car engineering that it is impossible to list them all here. Perhaps most importantly the 7 of 1934 popularized front wheel drive, a system very widely used today on all sizes of cars. But in those days it was a radical step, even for André Citroën who was known for his advanced thinking on car design. Citroën cared little about how much it would cost to solve the complex problem of driving *and* steering the front wheels and, on the prototype cars, added the further complication of automatic transmission (later abandoned). The other significant advance in the Model 7 was the adoption of a unitary or monococque body construction – the forerunner of the modern method of making motor cars using welded panels. The *Traction Avant* (it means front-wheel drive in French) enjoyed a remarkably long production run; it was on the market between 1934 and 1957 when it was replaced by the DS/ID series saloons. During its long history a considerable number of variants were produced, including the rare convertible. The 15/6 saloon was the first to use the famous Citroën oleopneumatic suspension system, but on the rear wheels only. This milestone motor car almost cost André Citroën his company, it brought Citroën close to bankruptcy, and certainly cost him his health because he died shortly before it went into production.

1952 Volkswagen Beetle

Volkswagen Beetle

The name *Volkswagen* in German means literally 'People's Car'. It was Adolf Hitler, then Chancellor of Germany, who in 1934 decided that it would be a good idea for the state to make a cheap car that almost everyone could afford to buy. The Beetle was designed by Dr Ferdinand Porsche and was very different from most other cars of the day, with its strange humped shape, from which it got its nickname. The engine, installed at the back, was an air-cooled flat four. Early cars had no rear window at all. The People's Car project never really got under way before Germany was overtaken by war and the factory at Wolfsburg was turned over to making military versions of the car. After the war, Ford was offered the chance to buy the plant, but turned it down and it was left to a British Army team to get things going again. The Beetle has proved to be one of the most successful designs ever. Production ceased only recently, after more than 20 million examples had been sold, in 30 countries throughout the world.

1959 and 1984 Minis

Mini
The Mini was born in 1959 and is still going strong. It looks set to join other long-running designs, such as the VW Beetle and the Citroën 2CV in the motoring hall of fame. Designed by Sir Alec Issigonis, this little car set new standards for the amount of interior space that could be provided within a compact overall size (the car is only three metres (10ft) long). The key to its success lay in the decision to position the engine sideways, across the frame and driving the front wheels. This meant that not only could the body design have a short nose, but also no interior space was lost to the gearbox and transmission hump in the floor. Handling has always been a strong point with Minis, and led to an illustrious sporting career, especially in rallies and saloon car circuit racing where the little cars collected a large number of major prizes. Like the Beetle, the basic shape has hardly changed over the years, although later models were much more refined and better equipped. Variations included the famous Mini-Cooper, the first production Mini to use disc brakes, and the Clubman series with a new 'modern' front end. Current models have returned to the more familiar 'big mouth' front grille used on the Mk II models. There are two estate versions, the Countryman, with timber decoration or plain steel panels. Hydrolastic suspension was tried for some years, but later cars reverted to the original rubber cone system.

◀ **The control yoke** and instrument read-out.

Mazda MX-03

The time has come when the so-called 'Concept Cars', put on display by car companies at international motor shows, have stopped being pure flights of fancy. This is because so many of these cars have features that are due to appear very shortly on production models. MX-03, from the Japanese Mazda company, has many interesting design features, including a triple rotor rotary engine, and steering that operates on front and rear wheels. The engine and turbocharger use a number of parts made from ceramic, a material which the engineers have found to be better than metal at resisting high temperatures. In addition to four-wheel steering (already being pursued by a number of other carmakers) the MX-03 has a transmission driving all four wheels and special anti-skid braking system, although these two features are now becoming widely available on a number of more conventional cars. Inside, the MX-03 has no steering wheel, instead the driver uses an aircraft-style control yoke. The instrument read-out is projected on to the windscreen in front of the driver so that he does not have to take his eyes from the road while checking the speed or other readings.

Honda/Williams Formula One

The most glamorous section of motor sport is Grand Prix racing, or Formula One as it is called. Frequent changes in rules, especially reductions in engine size, are designed to prevent cars going so fast. But even though many of the tracks are not good enough, average speeds have risen to such an extent that 321km/h (200mph) is not an unusual performance for a competitive car such as the Canon Williams Honda shown here. Powered by a turbocharged Honda racing engine, the car won the 1986 Constructors title and one of the team drivers, Nigel Mansell, almost took the world driver championship. Although they may look fragile, these single-seaters have to be very tough to resist the strains and stresses of racing. High tech materials are used, including strong but lightweight plastic composite materials such as Kevlar to build the main bodywork, called 'the tub' because it looks like a bathtub. The FWII 1986 car had a twin turbocharger, 1.5 litre Honda V6 engine, and a six-speed Williams gearbox. It was 279cm (110in) long, a maximum 180cm (71in) wide but stood only 89cm (35in) high. It carried fire extinguishers in the cockpit, and a separate air supply for the driver. Cockpit controls included adjustment levers for the brake balance, turbo boost, switches for the radio link with the pits, and a built-in drinks dispenser.

Thrust 2

This jet-powered car is the current holder of the World Land Speed Record title. In October 1983, Englishman Richard Noble completed two runs in the Black Rock desert, Nevada, USA, averaging a speed of 1019.76km/h (633.67mph) to beat the 13-year-old record held by Gary Gabelich of the USA with his liquid fuel rocket car 'Blue Flame'. Before the advent of the jet cars, record breakers were powered in a more conventional way, with the engine or engines driving the wheels. Now to reach even higher speeds the cars are propelled by the thrust of the jet efflux, like an aircraft. Such high speeds mean that record cars cannot rely on ordinary braking systems to stop, and they have to use braking parachute systems from jet fighter planes. Apart from being very risky, record breaking is also extremely expensive and Noble needed sponsorship from 200 companies to support his successful attempt. The power unit for Thrust was a Rolls-Royce Avon 302 from a jet-fighter aircraft. It produced the equivalent of 34,000 horsepower at full thrust, at which point it consumed over five gallons of aviation fuel per second. The driver, sitting in a cramped cockpit, had to think very fast indeed because at record-breaking speeds Thrust covered 1.6km (1 mile) every 5.5 seconds. This was one reason why the controls were kept fairly simple, with an aircraft-style steering yoke which also carried the firing buttons for the two sets of braking parachutes.

Richard Noble with 'Thrust 2'

How It Works

Let's look at how a car works. We'll begin by examining the layout, which in most cars means the body, made from specially pressed steel panels that are welded together to make a strong box. The engine, which we will examine in detail later, is usually positioned at the front, although some cars such as the famous Volkswagen Beetle and the Porsche sports cars, place it at the back. Ferrari and the Pontiac Fiero are examples of cars which have the engine in the middle of the car. This gives a perfect distribution of weight, but leaves little room for more than two people.

To make the road wheels turn, you need a system to link them to the engine. Early cars used belts and chains, but they kept breaking. These days steel shafts are used. They run from the gearbox which contains up to five different gears that operate a bit like a bicycle gear system, allowing the cyclist or driver to select the best compromise between the effort from his legs, or the car engine, and the road speed.

In most cars only the rear pair of wheels used to be driven, and the car was, in effect, *pushed* along. Later, designers decided to try driving the front wheels instead, so that the car was *pulled* around. This is

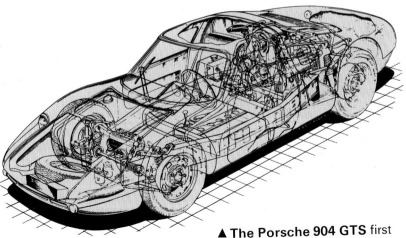

◀ **Feverish activity around** the Jaguar Sports Group C racing car.

▲ **The Porsche 904 GTS** first appeared in 1964, and shows the famous Porsche rear engine/rear drive layout.

currently the most popular choice for all but very large cars, although there is a growing trend for the manufacturers to offer buyers the option of having all four wheels driven, like a Second World War Jeep or a Land Rover. This began in motor sport with the rally teams who discovered the many advantages of all-wheel-drive.

The steering wheel controls the direction of the car and it has been a wheel for many years, although some early cars and steamers used a tiller like a boat. But someone will always try to change things and on many of the special designer cars at motor shows you can see some

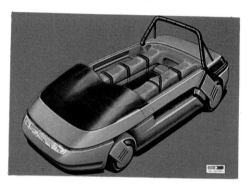

◀ **Giorgio Giugiaro's** amazing machine, Machimoto.

▶ **The 'steering wheel'** on the Pontiac Pursuit car is in fact a complex control pad which contains all the controls, including an in-car telephone and travel guide system.

amazing alternatives, although not many of them are very practical. Italian designer Giorgio Giugiaro once produced a machine called Machimoto that was a mixture of car and motorcycle. The driver and passengers sat inside the 'car' on long saddles, and the driver used a pair of handlebars to steer it. In more conventional cars the steering wheel acts on the front wheels through a shaft and gear system, and some of the more expensive cars these days have power assistance to take the hard work out of it. In the next few years more cars will be

INSIDE A CAR

If you were to peel off the shiny skin of a modern car, this is what it might look like. This cut-away of the latest 7-series saloon from BMW shows how every square inch of space not needed for passengers and luggage is filled with the complex components that are needed for a smooth and trouble-free ride. Like so many cars in this class, the big BMW relies extensively upon electronics feeding information to computer 'brains' to handle such things as making the engine perform efficiently, taking over the braking in an emergency to avoid a skid, and even telling the driver when the car needs a service. The metal shell is specially built to absorb the impacts in an accident and keep passengers safe in the central core of the body.

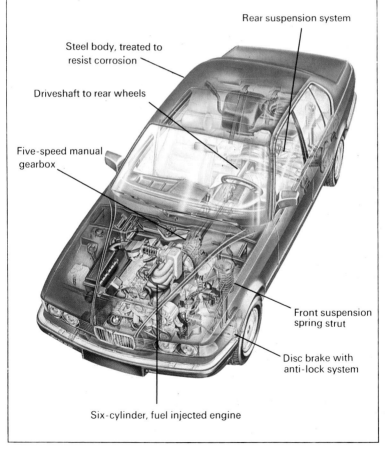

Rear suspension system

Steel body, treated to resist corrosion

Driveshaft to rear wheels

Five-speed manual gearbox

Front suspension spring strut

Disc brake with anti-lock system

Six-cylinder, fuel injected engine

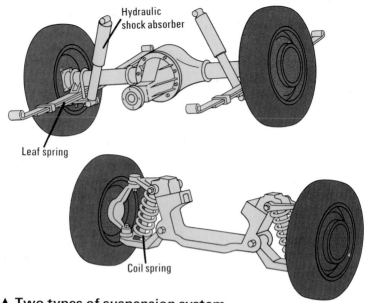

▲ Two types of suspension system, leaf springs and coil springs. The hydraulic shock absorber helps to cushion the effect of the car going over a bump.

appearing with four-wheel steering – that means the back pair of wheels will be steerable as well, for better cornering.

However well they are looked after the roads are never perfectly smooth, and the car does need to have some springs, so that the passengers can have a comfortable ride, and the car is not impossible to control. Early cars used large coach springs, but they were too soft. Leaf springs, layers of steel strip bolted together and used to link the axle and the bodywork, are still used but the most modern solution is a coil spring which works on each wheel so that it can move independently of the others. These steel springs are sometimes replaced with gas cylinders or the clever Hydrolastic system used on the Austin and Morris 1100 cars which had special water-filled springs. Citroën still uses a similar but more successful hydro-pneumatic arrangement in the CX and BX models. The British sports car firm Lotus and General Motors of America are close to perfecting a computer-controlled suspension system that allows the car to 'read' the road ahead through special sensors, and adjust the suspension for the best ride and performance.

Let's not forget the tyres. Early motorists rode on spoked carriage type wheels with solid rubber tyres. No wonder those early cars were called boneshakers! It was not until the turn of the century that inflatable tyres became available. Modern tyres are capable of handling very high speeds and tough conditions.

Of course it is all very well to start the car, but how do you stop it? The old-fashioned brake used to slow down a horse-drawn carriage was not really up to the job of stopping a car and so a whole new technology was developed. Again it was racing that helped to improve the situation. Carriage brakes used blocks, usually of wood, which were pressed against the wheel rim by a lever. The early motorists tried leather straps which were tightened around a drum. Next came brakes with special metal segments, lined with heat resistant friction material that could be expanded inside the drum. These last to the present day, although a majority of cars use modern disc brakes on at least one axle. Disc brakes, developed by the racing Jaguars and the aircraft industry, use a steel disc that rotates with the wheel and which is stopped by a pair of powerful callipers lined with friction material which nip the disc.

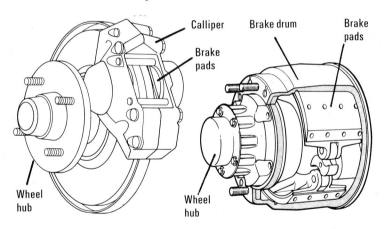

▲ **Disc brakes** are found on many modern cars. The brake pads are held on either side of the metal disc by a powerful calliper. The disc is prevented from overheating by the flow of air around the wheel.

▲ **Air brakes** are larger brakes usually found on trucks. They use air pressure instead of the fluid (hydraulic) pressure which operates disc brakes. When the brake is pressed a valve opens and releases the air.

THE V12 ENGINE

The new BMW V12 engine is due to make its appearance in the latest 7-Series cars. Large engines are back in fashion again now that their fuel consumption can be controlled by electronic management systems; they used to be called 'gas guzzlers'. There is no doubt that an eight- or twelve-cylinder powerplant is better balanced and much smoother than a smaller engine, which would have to work much harder to produce anything like the same output.

The component parts of the BMW V12 are produced by machines running under computer control, which are extremely accurate. This in turn means that the engine should be more reliable. As this engine is a V12, you will see that there are 12 pistons and connecting rods, and six combustion chambers in each of the two cylinder heads.

▲ **The Jaguar C-type** sports/racing car gives a perfect demonstration of the way in which motor racing has improved the design of cars. Jaguar pioneered the development of disc brakes, fitting them to the C-type entered for the 1952 Mille Miglia race. At that time all cars were using brake drums which quickly overheated and as a result were less efficient. But the idea was not new – the famous engineer Frederick Lanchester had thought of it many years before.

The Engine

Back to the beginning and the engine. On page 20 you will find a diagram illustrating the principle of the four-stroke engine and how it develops its power inside the cylinder. That principle is still used today, but modern engines are much more powerful and efficient.

Engines can have any number of cylinders, but they are usually even numbers – 4, 6, 8, 12 or even 16 – for better balance, although Audi, for example, have a five-cylinder engine and Daihatsu a three-cylinder one. The cylinders can be arranged in line, but that can make the engine rather long and awkward to fit under the bodywork, so, for eight cylinders and above the engine is often split into two, as a V8 (four on each side), V12 (six on each side) and so on. Some engines have the cylinders laid flat on opposite sides. They are called 'boxer' engines, the most famous of which is Ferrari.

The fuel and air mixture is metered by using a carburettor. This maintains the mixture balance so that the engine can draw in what it needs to make the explosion that provides the power. These days more cars are moving over to fuel injection, which is exactly what it sounds like – exactly measured squirts of fuel directly into the combustion chamber, the system usually controlled by an electronic brain that automatically adjusts the amounts to the demands made by the driver through the accelerator.

Ignition, the time at which the spark plug fires and ignites the charge of fuel and air, can be controlled by a mechanical distributor driven by the engine itself, but today – as with fuel injection – electronics are taking over and the job is done by a little black box. Diesels do not have spark plugs, but they do have injection systems. They work on a different principle, relying on squeezing up the charge to high pressure, thereby generating so much heat that it ignites by itself.

▶ **A closer look at a cylinder.** As the piston moves up and down, the connecting rod turns the crankshaft in a circular motion. Through other shafts this turning motion eventually makes its way to the wheels.

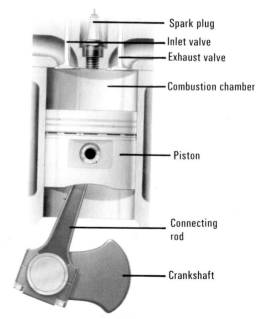

Spark plug

Inlet valve

Exhaust valve

Combustion chamber

Piston

Connecting rod

Crankshaft

▶ **This machine is making a microchip** – a thin wafer of material coated with a microscopic network of wires which carry signals through the complex circuits of a computer. Microchips are now used extensively in cars to control many functions; engine levels, information for the driver and even navigation.

Electronics

One of the biggest revolutions in modern car design started with the arrival of the microchip. This incredible piece of electronic wizardry has given us computers small enough to be strapped to the wrist but with a capability equalling machines which, only 20 years ago, would have occupied an entire room. The application of computer technology to the motor car has provided both the engineer and the designer with the equivalent of a new set of tools, helping to make cars more efficient and easier to drive.

Today there are big worries about the possible harm to people and their environment caused by noxious fumes from traffic. Governments all over the world are examining ways of cutting down on this pollution. Making everyone switch to electric power would be one method, but a more realistic way is to clean up the engines of cars and trucks. The microchip helps by allowing much finer control of the engine. Some of the more expensive cars have sophisticated boxes of electronics, capable of making the engine perform at its peak level under almost any conditions, and so reducing unnecessary pollution.

Future cars will use electronics for controlling suspension systems, relaying information to the driver, controlling the atmosphere inside the car and navigating the car. Some of these features are already being introduced. Lotus, Volvo and General Motors are working on

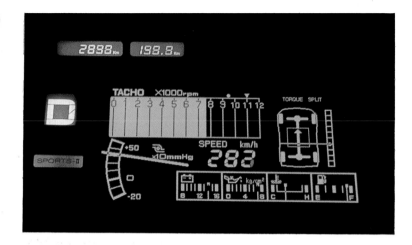

▲ This kind of electronic dashboard

appears in a number of cars available now.
There is a variable display, like a digital
watch, so that drivers can call up the
readout they wish to see by pressing a
button.

a new kind of suspension system that is capable of 'reading' the road ahead. It assesses the demands to be made on the springing and sets up to meet them. Production is not far away.

But engine management is now almost old hat – Volkswagen has had its 'plug-in' engine diagnostics system for many years. The real advances are being made in instrument displays and information relay to the driver, borrowing heavily from the research done in aircraft and space technology. This includes features such as holographic displays – projections of images which appear to hang in mid-air. This is especially useful if you want to avoid the driver having to look down at the instrument panel too often. The image of the speedometer is projected on to an area of the windscreen, and the driver does not have to take his eyes from the road for a second (*see page 39*).

Such a system is included in the Pontiac Pursuit, shown here, which is a working example of how a car on sale in the year 2000 may look. But it is worth remembering that many of the features it offers are already available, such as 'memory seats' which can be programmed to remember settings for the cushion tilt, backrest rake, height, distance from the steering wheel etc. Get in, punch in your code, and the seat is set up to fit you perfectly. Although the Pursuit does have the holographic instrument projection one thing it does not have is a conventional steering wheel. Instead there is a pair of handgrips operating what Pontiac calls a 'driver interface unit' (*see page 44*). What this means is that almost all the controls, including steering of course, are incorporated into this single unit, which relies on electronics for control.

There is a navigation system to work out the best route, and an amazing communications device incorporating a telephone which can dial pre-programmed numbers to give the driver information about hotels, restaurants and filling stations in the area, as well as his own personal diary of events and appointments. Mirrors are old-fashioned when it comes to seeing what is going on outside the Pursuit vehicle. It uses small television cameras which project the image on to TV screens inside the car. Of course, back seat passengers are not expected to make do with boring old radio or cassette players, they can plug into the car's hi-tech hi-fi with compact disc stereo, or look at the colour televisions.

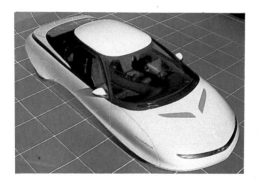

◀ **The smooth shape of the Pontiac Pursuit** car means that it is extremely aerodynamic and quiet. Instead of normal headlights the Pursuit has a light 'bar' extending across the front.

▶ **The interior of the Pontiac Pursuit** is called 'organic' by the designers. Its rounded, soft shapes are meant to make the driver feel at home and relaxed.

Navigation

The invention of the compact disc player is making life a lot easier for the modern motorist who can use it as a kind of 'talking map' to find the best way to his or her destination, or to avoid queues in traffic jams. This is just one example of how the electronics revolution is moving in on motoring.

Finding your way around was fairly easy in the early days, chiefly because there were not very many roads on which to get lost. In any case, the chance of making the journey without a breakdown or a puncture was fairly remote and so there was plenty of time to think about where you were going. The roads of the time were the main routes between towns followed by the carriages and the mail coaches. Once off these main routes the pioneer motorist found himself on country roads, little more than cart tracks, which were so rutted and bumpy that his car could be shaken to bits after only a few miles.

As cars became more popular and more reliable, the road systems were expanded and improved, maps became more complex, and cross-country navigation required quite a bit of careful planning beforehand. Today, in Europe especially, the problem is that roads

▼ The Peugeot Proxima project car has a three-dimensional projector for navigational information, and five video display units to show data from the two on-board compters.

▲ Renault's navigation system is called ATLAS, short for 'Acquisition by Telediffusion of Automobile Logistics for Services'. It includes information about hotels, restaurants and tourism.

are grossly overloaded. Motorways and main roads help relieve smaller roads of through traffic, but in overcrowded towns and cities, driving can be a nightmare. Not only are the roads packed with traffic, but the situation is changing all the time, and an accident or a broken down vehicle can cause instant paralysis of the system, leaving hundreds of people sitting in traffic jams.

This is where the CD system comes in. Because it is capable of storing a vast amount of information in a small space, the CD can be loaded with all the road data of a major city such as London or New York. This information can be played back on to a video screen or through the radio system as a kind of 'voice map'. It will cost a good deal more than a paper map, but then an ordinary map cannot talk you out of a jam the way a CD system can. You tell it where you are and where you want to go, and it will talk you through the journey. Special sensors linked into the car mileometer calculate where you are and trigger the system to tell you which way to turn and when.

In its ultimate form, the system can be plugged in to the radio traffic warning network and store information about jams and accidents that may affect your progress, and then work out an alternative route around them. You can use it while listening to your favourite programme or music, because the system is trained to be polite, and interrupts only when it needs to provide a direction!

Sports Cars/Convertibles

BMW 325i Convertible　D

Most big European car makers use specialist coachbuilders from outside to produce their convertibles. BMW does the job itself, building the car from the wheels upwards. A neat design for the hood allows it to be folded away out of sight under a steel panel behind the rear seats, and a triple layer top makes the car snug in bad weather. The six-cylinder, 2.5 litre engine gives the 325i a brilliant performance, with very good handling and ride.

Max speed: 215km/h (134mph)
Length: 432cm (170in)
Weight: 1252kg (2761lb)

Caterham Super Seven　GB

Designed in the late 1950s by Colin Chapman, the man who created Lotus, the Seven is still going strong. It is an out and out sports two-seater, with little weather protection. Emphasis is very much on handling – but not ride – and performance, which can be shattering with the optional 150bhp Ford BDR engine. Even with a standard 84bhp engine in this tiny car the acceleration is still outstanding. A car for the hardy!

Max speed: 160km/h (100mph)
Length: 338cm (133in)
Weight: 509kg (1122lb)

Porsche 959

Is this the ultimate sports car? There may be a passing resemblance to the 27-year-old 911, but under the skin it is very different. The flat six 'boxer' engine has air-cooled cylinder barrels, but water-cooled cylinder heads. Add a turbocharger, and the 2.9 litre engine produces an amazing 450bhp. Permanent four-wheel drive is needed to put all this power down on to the road. The 959 looks very like many of the racing Porsches and this is not entirely coincidental. Even with its excellent aerodynamic shaping, at the speeds it can achieve the 959 needs the large wing on the back, to prevent it from becoming a real flier!

Rear engine, four-wheel drive. Six cylinders, 2850cc; 450bhp at 6500rpm.
Max speed: Over 299km/h (186mph)
Length: 442cm (174in)
Weight: 1417kg (3124lb)

Jaguar XJ SC Cabrio (GB)

The open top version of the famous XJ-S coupé, this is a refined, classically British sports car. The hard 'Targa' top can be lifted off and stowed in the boot, and the flexible rear hood section folds down neatly. It is produced with either the big 5.3 litre V12 engine or the 3.6 litre AJ6 engine also used in the new XJ-6 saloon.

Max speed: 241km/h (150mph)
Length: 477cm (188in)
Weight: 1796kg (3960lb)

Lotus Esprit Turbo (GB)

A low, wide and good looking two-seater, with a moulded plastic body designed by the Italian company, Giugiaro. The central steel backbone chassis carries a mid-mounted engine and suspension pick-up points, and the 2.2 litre, four-cylinder engine is turbocharged to produce 218bhp. A very fast car with safe handling and smooth, comfortable ride.

Max speed: 245km/h (152mph)
Length: 429cm (169in)
Weight: 1197kg (2640lb)

Morgan 4/4 (GB)

There is still a long waiting list for this classic British sports car which has remained almost unchanged since the 1930s. The separate chassis has unique sliding pillar front suspension and the body is still made with ash frames, now protected against woodworm. There is also a 2 + 2 version.

Front engine, rear drive. Four cylinders, 1598cc; 96bhp at 6000rpm.
Max speed: 185km/h (115mph)
Length: 366cm (144in)
Weight: 733kg (1617lb)

Reliant SS1 Turbo (GB)

A small open two-seater, with separate steel chassis and moulded plastic bodywork. The headlamps lie flat and pop up when in use. The Turbo version is powered by the 1.8 litre engine from the Nissan Silvia. The SS1 has replaced the much larger Scimitar produced by this specialist English manufacturer.

Front engine, rear drive. Four cylinders, 1809cc; 135bhp at 6000rpm.
Max speed: 178km/h (111mph)
Length: 388cm (153in)
Weight: 838kg (1848lb)

TVR 390 SE Convertible GB

A high performance open two-seater powered by an aluminium 3.9 litre version of the Rover engine. It has a separate and very strong tubular steel chassis; with independent suspension at front and rear, and the sleek bodywork is moulded in glass fibre. Together with its distinctive short trunk and flush hood line, it has a deep front air dam, and built-in extra driving lamps.

Front engine, rear drive. V8, 3907cc; 270bhp at 5500rpm.
Max speed: 241km/h (150mph)
Length: 409cm (161in)
Weight: 1127kg (2486lb)

De Tomaso Pantera ⓘ

The last of the US-engined Italian 'super cars', launched at the 1970 New York motor show. A mid-mounted 5.8 litre Ford 8 supplies the power for this two-seater coupé with a Ghia body. A low, rather aggressive-looking car, it provides very good performance and handling.

Mid engine, rear drive. V8, 5769cc; 270bhp at 5600rpm.
Max speed: 249km/h (155mph)
Length: 427cm (168in)
Weight: 1417kg (3124lb)

Ferrari Testarossa (I)

The reason this car is called the 'Red Head'? Open the bonnet and you will see that the cylinder heads on the flat 12 engine have a bright red finish. This model with its very distinctive 'slatted' body styling, replaced the BB512 at the 1984 Paris Salon where it was first seen. The 4.9 litre mid-mounted engine has twin overhead camshafts, operating four valves per cylinder and standard power output is 390bhp, boosted to 470bhp for the Group B racing version. Its performance is outstanding and the handling everything you might expect from a car bearing the famous Prancing Horse badge. It is only a two-seater and luggage space is strictly limited, but you would not expect to collect the groceries in a car like this!

Mid engine, rear drive. Flat 12, 4942cc; 390bhp at 6300rpm.
Max speed: 290km/h (180mph)
Length: 449cm (177in)
Weight: 1500kg (3311lb)

61

Lamborghini Countach

The can be no mistaking this fabulous looking Italian two-seater coupé, designed by coach-builders Bertone. The doors do not open outwards but upwards, while the big air scoops above the rear wheels supply radiators and oil coolers. The V12 engine has four valves per cylinder – which is why the word 'quattrovalvole' appears by the car's name on the engine cover. American versions have petrol injection rather than the six Weber twin choke carburettors. Its performance is quite stunning – from a standstill to 96.5km/h (60mph) in just 4.9 seconds, and a top speed of 286km/h (178mph). The handling is well able to cope with these sort of speeds, with massive ventilated disc brakes to make sure that the car can stop as well as it can go.

Mid engine, rear wheel drive. V12, 5167cc; 455bhp at 7000rpm.
Max speed: 286km/h (178mph)
Length: 376cm (148in)
Weight: 1487kg (3278lb)

Maserati Biturbo Spyder (I)

A relatively new model in a range which should change the fortunes of this famous car maker. The car's name gives away its secret: unlike most other turbocharged cars, the Biturbo uses not one but two turbos, one feeding each bank of the 2.0 litre V6 engine. This engine is fairly conventional with three valves per cylinder, but Maserati now has a version with no less than six valves. There are four versions of the car including two and four door models, making it the staple product of the factory. The convertibles are built by the famous coachbuilder, Zagato, the 2 + 2 car having clean but conservative lines without the usual addition of a roll-over bar to spoil the look.

Cadillac Allante (USA)

This car has what must be the longest production line in the world, starting in Turin, Italy and finishing at Hamtramck, Michigan. General Motors wanted a European-styled car to compete with the Mercedes-Benz SL range, so it looked to top Italian company Pininfarina as a partner. The body was created and crash tested in Italy, while Cadillac designed the transverse 4.1 litre V8 engine to drive the front wheels. The bodies are built and painted in Italy and then flown in specially converted Alitalia Boeing 747s to Detroit, 56 at a time, three times a week, where the engines and running gear are fitted. The open two-seater has a hard top which can be quickly fitted when needed.

Front engine, rear drive. V6, 1995cc; 205bhp at 6500rpm.
Max speed: 215km/h (134mph)
Length: 403cm (159in)
Weight: 1083kg (2387lb)

Front engine, front drive. V8 4100cc; 170bhp at 4300rpm.
Max speed: 199km/h (124mph)
Length: 454cm (179in)
Weight: 1584kg (3493lb)

63

Excalibur Series V (USA)

Remarkable 'replicar' based, loosely, on the huge Mercedes-Benz 500/540K models of the late 1930s. But there its resemblance ends. The Series V is powered by a 5.0 litre Chevrolet V8 engine, which drives the rear wheels through four-speed Hydra-Matic automatic transmission. There is even independent suspension at the rear and the Series V has a proper, separate ladder-type chassis, with aluminium bodywork. Despite limited output the Excalibur has survived since 1964.

Max speed: 180km/h (112mph)
Length: 518cm (204in)
Weight: 2095kg (4620lb)

Ford Mustang GT

The Mustang has come a long way since the original and highly successful model which first appeared in the early 1960s. The current GT is a much smaller, compact car, with distinctive sloping bonnet and recessed headlamps. Standard engines are the 120bhp V6 and the 200bhp 4.9 litre V8, with the 88bhp, 2.3 litre four-cylinder an option. The convertible version of the Mustang GT is currently Ford's only soft top model in production.

Max speed: 175km/h (109mph)
Length: 454cm (179in)
Weight: 1227kg (2706lb)

Mazda RX7 *(left)*

Mazda is the only manufacturer in the world to continue to develop and use the Wankel rotary piston engine. Millions of dollars have been spent in developing the engine to meet the strict Japanese and US exhaust emissions regulations. The RX7 – or the Savanna – has a twin rotor unit, driving the rear wheels through a five-speed gearbox. As you can see from the picture it has a sleek fastback 2 + 2 coupé body, with pop-up headlamps. For US versions, a special rear suspension was developed, which aimed for a more comfortable ride rather than for ultimate handling. To compensate for the power loss caused by fitting catalytic converter emission control equipment, US and Japanese market cars are offered with turbochargers. Overall design closely follows that of the Porsche 944.

Front engine, rear drive. Twin rotor, 2616cc; 148bhp at 6500rpm.
Max speed: 209km/h (130mph)
Length: 432cm (170in)
Weight: 1222kg (2695lb)

Ford RS200 **GB**

This fantastic car was created to do just one job – win the World Rally Championship. Unfortunately it did not and, with the banning of the Group B rally 'super cars', it will never have the opportunity to do so again. Only 200 were ever built, and it costs around 750,000 dollars to buy one! For that you get a tiny cockpit just able to hold two people. There is barely enough boot space to carry a toothbrush – but in full rally trim, this car can hurtle from a standstill to 96.5km/h (60mph) in just 2.6 seconds. Its power comes from a turbocharged, 1.8 litre four-cylinder engine which produces 250bhp. The drive is through all four wheels, to give the traction necessary for loose surfaces. The handling and grip is phenomenal, while the ride is surprisingly good for what is, after all, a competition car. Ford did produce a few special RS200s, complete with leather trim and electric windows!

Mid engine, four-wheel drive.
  Four cylinders, 1803cc;
  250bhp at 6500rpm.
Max speed: 225km/h
  (140mph)
Length: 401cm (158in)
Weight: 1177kg (2596lb)

Chrysler Maserati USA

Lke GM with the Allante, Chrysler has co-operated with an Italian company to produce a new model. The open 2 + 2 body and the car's suspension were developed by Maserati, while the power train is supplied by Chrysler. The 2.2 litre four-cylinder turbo engine, driving the front wheels, produces 174bhp.

Max speed: 209km/h (130mph)
Length: 447cm (176in)
Weight: 1372kg (3025lb)

Panther Kallista 2.8i GB

Although it looks like a 1930s sports car, the Kallista is not based on any particular model. The aluminium body is made in Korea, and then shipped to Britain. Suspension components come from the obsolete Ford Cortina Mk.V, while the Kallista is powered by a petrol injection version of the Ford V6 engine.

Max speed: 198km/h (123mph)
Length: 388cm (153in)
Weight: 898kg (1980lb)

Performance Hatchbacks

Peugeot 205 Turbo 16

It may look like an ordinary 205 from the outside, but under the skin it is very different. It has a tubular steel chassis/body frame, clad with lightweight body panels, and instead of the engine being at the front, it is offset to one side where the back seats would be if the car had any. The 1.8 litre four-cylinder engine has 16 valves which together with an inter-cooled turbocharger produce 200bhp in standard form and 450bhp when tuned up for competition use. For the Group B model much of the bodywork is moulded in Kevlar. There is, of course, four-wheel drive to get all this power down on to the road. The special Paris-Dakar Rally version was 28cm (11in) longer than the standard, with a massive 1183 litre (118 gallon) fuel tank. The trio of works-entered 205/T16s are also due to take part in the Baja 1000 off-road rally.

Mid engine, four-wheel drive.
  Four cylinders, 1775cc;
  200bhp at 6750rpm.
Max speed: 209km/h (130mph)
Length: 381cm (150in)
Weight: 1142kg (2519lb)

Ford Escort XR3i

The fastest and most powerful version of the production European Escorts. A fuel injection 1.6 litre engine, plus stiffened suspension give the car a sports car-like performance with a hatchback capacity.

Max speed: 185km/h (115mph)
Length: 406cm (160in)
Weight: 823kg (1815lb)

VW Golf GTi

The first of the European 'hot hatchbacks', developed 11 years ago. The standard version has a 1.8 litre, eight valve cylinder head, but there is now a much more powerful, 139bhp model with twin overhead camshafts and four valves per cylinder. Flared wheel arches and low profile tyres give the GTi a sporting look.

Front engine, front drive. Four cylinders, eight valve 112bhp at 5500rpm; 16 valve 139bhp at 6100rpm.
Max speeds: 186km/h/ 207km/h (116mph/ 129mph)
Length: 388cm (153in)
Weight: 863kg (1903lb)

MG Metro Turbo

The chunky little Metro follows in the footsteps of the famous Mini-Coopers, with a turbo version of the same 1275cc transverse engine. The power has been deliberately kept down to 94bhp to conserve the four-speed gearbox which is located in the engine oil pan. Performance is lagging a bit when compared to newer rivals, but handling is still legendary.

Max speed: 180km/h (112mph)
Length: 340cm (134in)
Weight: 793kg (1749lb)

Opel Kadett GSI

The aerodynamic bodywork of this three-door family hatchback gives it an amazingly high top speed. Power comes from a 1.8 litre single overhead cam engine, driving the front wheels through a five-speed gearbox. The GSI version has a deeper front air dam, and rear wing to help stability.

Front engine, front drive. Four cylinder, 1796cc; 115bhp at 5800rpm.
Max speed: 202km/h (126mph)
Length: 398cm (157in)
Weight: 838kg (1848lb)

Mazda 323 4 × 4 Turbo

The familiar Mazda 323 takes on a new appearance with this high powered, four-wheel drive version which looks like having an exciting future in competitions. The sixteen valve 1.6 litre transverse engine drives all four wheels, giving superb traction in difficult conditions. Ride has been stiffened up to produce even better handling.

Max speed: 199km/h (124mph)
Length: 398cm (157in)
Weight: 863kg (1903lb)

Renault 5GT Turbo

This version of the little Renault 5 really looks the part, with flared plastic wheel arches and side skirts, a deep air dam and lowered suspension. The turbo version of the 1.4 litre engine drives the front wheels only and gives delightful handling, precise steering and excellent grip, making this a car which it is very easy to drive quickly.

Max speed: 230km/h (143mph)
Length: 358cm (141in)
Weight: 828kg (1826lb)

Estate Cars/Station Wagons

Ford Sierra 4 × 4 (GB)

The four-wheel drive system is not designed for ultimate performance, but rather to give a 'go almost anywhere' capability in snow and mud. Power comes from the 2.0 litre injection engine, with a five-speed gearbox.

Max speed: 190km/h (118mph)
Length: 452cm (178in)
Weight: 1162kg (2563lb)

Montego Estate (GB)

The Rover Group has dropped the Austin name for the Montego. A big capacity estate, with rearward facing, foldaway child seats an option. The standard engine is 1.6 litre, but there is also a 2.0 litre unit.

Max speed: 165km/h (103mph)
Length: 447cm (176in)
Weight: 1017kg (2244lb)

Renault Espace

This distinctive slope-fronted people carrier is not as straightforward as it might appear: rather than having the usual metal shell body, the Espace uses a steel 'skeleton' clad with a variety of moulded plastic panels, which can be easily replaced if they get damaged. Even the roof is a plastic laminate. Inside there are three rows of seats. The front pair can be swivelled round to face rearwards, while the centre two can be folded to make a table. The rear seats can also be folded out of the way to make room for a lot of luggage – and more can be stowed on the built-in roof rack. There are three engine options, starting with the 2.0 litre petrol version, and going on to the ordinary and turbo-diesel power units, all driving the front wheels.

Front engine, front drive. Four cylinders, 1995cc; 110bhp at 5500rpm.
Max speed: 175km/h (109mph)
Length: 424cm (167in)
Weight: 1222kg (2695lb)

Volvo 740GLE Estate

The estate car version of the Volvo 700 range looks very much less awkward than the sedan, a big, squared-up load carrier which can swallow a huge volume. The big 2.3 litre four-cylinder fuel injection engine puts out 131bhp, driving the rear wheels through either a five-speed manual gearbox or four-speed automatic transmission. The manual gearbox is unusual: it is a normal four-speed one, with a separate overdrive unit mounted at the back, operating on fourth gear only. This overdrive can be switched in or out by a button in the gear lever knob but if the lever is moved out of fourth, the overdrive is automatically disengaged. The squared up rear of the car, with the near-vertical tailgate, means that awkward items like freezers and furniture can be easily transported. As with all Volvo cars the design has been created with safety in mind (Volvo was one of the first manufacturers to install seat belts as standard). Some versions of this big estate car have special rearward-facing children's seats that can fold down into the floor of the boot.

Front engine, rear drive. Four cylinders, 2316cc; 131bhp at 5400rpm.
Max speed: 180km/h (112mph)
Length: 477cm (188in)
Weight: 1317kg (2904lb)

Chrysler LeBaron Town and Country

A compact, luxury version of the K-car. The Town and Country has the 2.5 litre version of the four-cylinder engine, driving the front wheels through a Torque-

flite automatic gearbox. Its distinctive feature is the 'half-timbered' trim on the body sides.

Max speed: 168km/h (105mph)
Length: 454cm (179in)
Weight: 1162kg (2563lb)

Mercedes-Benz 300TE

D

There are four versions of this estate car in the Mercedes W124 series. This one is powered by a 3.0 litre, six-cylinder engine with four-speed automatic gearbox fitted as standard, although a manual box can be ordered specially. It is spacious inside, and if the cavernous interior cannot take all the load, there is also a standard-fit roof rack. A roller net can be raised to section off the rear compartment when carrying pets.

Max speed: 213km/h (130mph)
Length: 476cm (187in)
Weight: 1550kg (3425lb)

Front engine, front drive. Four cylinders, 1488cc; 77bhp at 6000rpm.
Max speed: 159km/h (99mph)
Length: 398cm (157in)
Weight: 868kg (1914lb)

Honda Civic Shuttle

The tall styling means that the Shuttle is a very practical little people carrier, easy to get in and out of. A steeply sloping bonnet, and high seating position makes parking easy. The latest version is the Real Time which has semi-permanent four-wheel drive, drive to the rear wheels being automatically engaged when needed.

Front engine, front drive. Four cylinders, 213cc; 101bhp at 5600rpm.
Max speed: 148km/h (92mph)
Length: 447cm (176in)
Weight: 1320kg (2911lb)

Dodge Caravan

A practical, square-lined load carrier, with sloping bonnet and near vertical tailgate. The 2.2 litre transverse engine drives the front wheels. The long, 284cm (112in) wheelbase and low rear platform deck means that the Caravan can be used to transport big loads. An unusual feature is the vertical arrangement of the headlamps.

All Terrain Vehicles

Front engine, four-wheel drive. Four cylinders, 2299cc; 90bhp at 5000rpm.
Max speed: 143km/h (89mph)
Length: 396cm (156in) short wheelbase, 439cm (173in) long wheelbase
Weight: 1881kg (4147lb)

Mercedes-Benz 230GE **D**

This rugged cross country vehicle is a joint production between Mercedes-Benz in West Germany and Puch in Austria and known as a Puch in some countries. The mechanical parts are supplied from Germany and are assembled with the Austrian-built body at Graz. The permanent four-wheel drive has locking differentials front and rear.

Max speed: 140km/h (87mph)
Length: 444cm (175in)
Weight: 1862kg (4106lb)

Land Rover 110 Country **GB**

You can find Land Rovers throughout the world, tough and almost unbreakable. An immensely strong steel chassis carries the alloy body. The new 3.5 litre version has permanent four-wheel drive, with high and low ratio transfer boxes to allow it to tackle seemingly impossible conditions. Some Land Rovers nearly 40 years old are still in daily use.

Front engine, four wheel drive. V8, 3529cc; 125bhp at 4000rpm. Three-speed automatic transmission.
Max speed: 151km/h (94mph)
Length: 447cm (176in)
Weight: 1761kg (3883lb)

Range Rover Vogue GB

This big, comfortable ATV (All Terrain Vehicle) has only recently gone on sale in some areas of the United States, setting new standards in cross country ability. The V8 engine drives all four wheels through a three-speed automatic transmission, with locking differentials front and rear to give added traction in difficult conditions.

Lada Niva SU

Small and tough, this little ATV from the Soviet Union has a surprisingly high standard of trim and very good cross country ability. It has permanent four-wheel drive and a hard-working 1.6 litre engine.

Max speed: 132km/h (82mph)
Length: 370cm (146in)
Weight: 1149kg (2535lb)

Front engine, two- or four-wheel drive.
Four cylinders, 2464cc; 119bhp at 5000rpm.
Max speed: 135km/h (84mph)
Length: 386cm (152in)
Weight: 1272kg (2805lb)

AMC Jeep Wrangler

This new Jeep model is the successor to the famous CJ series. Like the original Jeep, the Wrangler is a relatively small ATV. There is a choice between 2.5 litre or 4.2 litre engines. Normal drive is through the rear wheels, with front-wheel drive added in bad conditions. Locking differentials can be fitted as extras.

Mitsubishi Pajero (J)

There are no fewer than 12 versions of this hard top ATV, with options of wagon or estate car bodies, and four engine ranges. There is a very strong box section chassis, with independent front suspension and a live axle at the rear. Normally only the rear wheels are driven, with the front wheels being brought into drive when the going gets tough.

Max speed: 135km/h (84mph)
Length: (LWB) 459cm (181in)
Weight: 1450kg (3197lb)

Lamborghini LM-002

It is hard to believe that the brutish and rugged LM-002 comes from the same factory as the sleek and low-slung Countach supercar, but then Lamborghini also build tractors and import wine! This must be the ultimate cross country car, with a powerful V12, 4.7 litre engine, derived from the sports car, which gives the LM-002 a potential maximum speed of 196km/h (122mph). Special puncture-proof tyres have been developed to withstand the punishment of high speed drives over rocky deserts. They are also self-sealing if hit by bullets. The body is plastic, fitted over a tubular frame.

Front engine, two- or four-wheel drive. V12, 4754cc; 332bhp at 6000rpm.
Max speed: 196km/h (122mph)
Length: 490cm (193in)
Weight: 2600kg (5733lb)

Toyota Land Cruiser

There are long and short wheel base versions of this tough ATV, with the options of petrol or diesel engines. It has a box section ladder-type chassis, and live axles front and rear, with rear-wheel drive being used under normal conditions. Freewheeling hubs on the front wheels reduce drive line drag and help fuel consumption. There is also an automatic transmission option.

Max speed: 154km/h (96mph)
Length: 474cm (187in) (LWB)
Weight: 1900kg (4189lb)

Suzuki SJ410

Also known as the Jimny, this little ATV is available in pick-up or hard top form. In Japan it can be bought with a tiny 539cc, 28bhp three-cylinder engine, but the 970cc, four-cylinder engine is more common elsewhere. It has permanent four wheel drive, with a low ratio transfer box to help when conditions are difficult.

Front engine, four-wheel drive. Four cylinders, 970cc; 52bhp at 6000rpm.
Max speed: 127km/h (79mph)
Length: 355cm (140in)
Weight: 758kg (1672lb)

Large Saloons

Rear engine, rear drive. V8, 3495cc; 168bhp at 5200rpm.
Max speed: 190km/h (118mph)
Length: 500cm (197in)
Weight: 1620kg (3572lb)

Tatra T613-2 (CS)

Unusual is the right word for this car. The mechanical layout dates back nearly 50 years, with the V8 engine hung out behind the rear axle line. To keep weight down, the engine is cooled by air rather than water. Swing axle rear suspension has been developed to make handling predictable, with rack and pinion steering. Its styling includes a four headlamp layout and no radiator grille.

Citroën CX 25 GTi Turbo (F)

Fastest and most powerful of the unique Citroën design, with oleopneumatic suspension, high pressure brakes and self centering power steering.

Max speed: 223km/h (139mph)
Length: 490cm (193in)
Weight: 1385kg (3054lb)

Renault 25 V6 Turbo (F)

The long wheelbase version of this luxury car is no longer produced. A hatchback design, with good handling and performance.

Max speed: 225km/h (140mph)
Length: 462cm (182in)
Weight: 1280kg (2822lb)

Audi 200 Avant quattro **D**

Audi started the move to permanent four-wheel drive in ordinary road-going cars. The Avant styling is a cross between a saloon and station wagon, with sloping tailgate. It has an unusual five-cylinder engine design, with five-speed gearbox. Locking differentials front and rear give added traction in snow and ice conditions. Its aerodynamic styling gives low drag.

Max speed: 223km/h (139mph)
Length: 480cm (189in)
Weight: 1450kg (3197lb)

Ford Granada Scorpio **D**

Recently the 2.8 litre V6 engine has been replaced by a 2.9 litre version, with cylinder heads designed to improve exhaust emission levels. Its smooth styling includes a hatchback tailgate for extra carrying capacity. Anti-lock braking is standard.

Max speed: 207km/h (129mph)
Length: 467cm (184in)
Weight: 1177kg (2596lb)

Mercedes-Benz 560 SEL (D)

This is the biggest Mercedes-Benz saloon, and is a worthy flagship for the S-class models produced by this famous manufacturer. The engine is a new 5.6 litre V8, made with lightweight aluminium alloy and linked to a four-speed gearbox which can be switched electronically between sport and economy shift programmes. Suspension is by hydropneumatics, instead of metal springing, and the driver can choose between a soft setting for cruising and a harder one for more sporting driving. Another device raises and lowers the riding height of the body according to road speed to improve aerodynamics. Inside, the car features a number of luxury touches including electrically controlled seat and steering column adjustment. The classic Mercedes-Benz three pointed star badge on the radiator is spring-loaded to fold up in the unfortunate event of an accident involving a pedestrian.

Front engine, rear drive, V8, 5547cc; 272bhp at 5000rpm.
Max speed: 228km/h (142mph)
Length: 528cm (208in)
Weight: 1866kg (4114lb)

Rover 800 Sterling **GB**

This is the British version of the co-operative venture between Rover and Honda. It is also the first Rover on the United States market since the 3500 in the mid-70s. The V6, 2.5 litre engine is a Honda designed unit, driving through the Honda automatic transmission. The body and suspension are British, with the system on the Sterling specifically developed for US conditions. A very high standard of equipment is offered, including anti-lock braking, air-conditioning, leather upholstery and wood veneer adding an air of traditional British craftsmanship. The Honda version of this car, called Legend, is a very close relative, although when they are viewed side by side there are quite distinct differences. Under a special deal between Austin Rover and Honda each company builds both cars. The British company sells both Hondas and Rovers in Britain, some parts of Europe, the USA and other markets, while Honda serve the Far East market. Austin Rover is considering the possibilities of developing a coupé version.

Front engine, front drive. V6, 2494cc; 151bhp at 5800rpm.
Max speed: 207km/h (129mph).
Length: 482cm (190in)
Weight: 1420kg (3131lb)

Bentley Mulsanne Turbo R GB

Rolls-Royce, who build the Bentley Turbo R, has never disclosed the power outputs of its engines, simply stating that they are 'sufficient'. But it does admit that the Turbo version produces fifty per cent more than the non-turbo injection version.

Max speed: 217km/h (135mph)
Length: 525cm (207in)
Weight: 2350kg (5181lb)

Jaguar XJ6 GB

It took Jaguar over six years to develop this new model. It may bear a passing resemblance to the previous version, but it is entirely new from radiator grille to rear fender. The new AJ6 engine first appeared in the XJ-S, and the 5.3 litre V12 version will be launched next year. Its brilliant handling combined with supple ride is in the Jaguar tradition, and the performance is everything expected of this famous firm as is the classic leather and wood trim. A feature of the car is the new design for the wiring system, which does away with the need for much of the bulky loom. Careful use is made of electronic displays for the warning systems.

Front engine, rear drive. Six cylinders, 3590cc; 221bhp at 5250rpm.
Max speed: 220km/h (137mph)
Length: 498cm (196in)
Weight: 1686kg (3719lb)

Rolls-Royce Silver Spirit

Recently Rolls-Royce made fuel injection standard on the Silver Spirit; in some countries carburettors were still being used. As with the Bentley Turbo R, no power outputs are quoted by the factory. Each car is built to an individual customer's requirements.

Max speed: 193km/h (120mph)
Length: 525cm (207in)
Weight: 2240kg (4939lb)

87

Mercury Sable

There is a strong family likeness here with the European Ford Scorpio, the main difference however, is under the bonnet. The Sable's engine drives the front rather than the rear wheels and there are options of 2.5 or 3.0 litre engines.

Max speed: 159km/h (99mph)
Length: 477cm (188in)
Weight: 1297kg (2860lb)

Opel Omega 3000 D

This is a brand new mid-range saloon, made by General Motors in Europe to replace the old Rekord and Vauxhall Carlton models. The 3000 is a top of the range sports car, which uses a powerful six-cylinder, 3.0 litre engine previously used in the bigger Senator and Monza cars. The suspension has been re-designed and is now completely independent. The 3000 is identified by spoilers, sideskirts and sports wheels.

Max speed: 209km/h (130mph)
Length: 468cm (184in)
Weight: 1178kg (2598lb)

Front engine, front
    drive. V6, 2966cc;
    127bhp at
    4900rpm.
Max speed:
    189km/h
    (118mph)
Length: 457cm
    (180in)
Weight: 1162kg
    (2563lb)

Buick Somerset T-type USA

This two-door saloon has a distinctive appearance, with a steeply raked windscreen and near-vertical rear window. The T-type is only available with a 3 litre, V6 engine, set transversely and driving the front wheels through a four-speed automatic transmission. The less sporting four-door variant of the Somerset is the Skylark.

Chrysler Fifth Avenue USA

Despite the trend towards more European styled medium-sized cars, larger American models tend to retain the classic limousine look exemplified here by the Fifth Avenue. Its windowless rear quarter accentuates the boxy look. The traditional powertrain includes a 5.5 litre, V8 engine driving the rear wheels through a three-speed Torqueflite automatic gearbox. The suspension is traditional too, with wishbones and a torsion bar at the front, and a rigid axle with semi-elliptic springs at the back.

Max speed: 180km/h (112mph)
Length: 523cm (206in)
Weight: 1696kg (3740lb)

Lincoln Continental USA

Lincoln is Ford's prestige marque, with all its models in the luxury range. The 4.9 litre engine has electronic fuel injection, driving the rear wheels through an automatic overdrive transmission. It has classic well-balanced sloping lines, and features the distinctive Lincoln radiator grille. Disc brakes are fitted to all four wheels, and of course power steering is standard.

Max speed: 249km/h (155mph)
Length: 510cm (201in)
Weight: 1711kg (3773lb)

Stutz Royale Limousine USA

The entire Stutz range is unusual. The lines seem to be sculptured, with mock outside exhaust pipes, spare wheel mounted on the boot and a long, overhanging front. It has a GM power unit and Turbo Hydra-Matic transmission, but like Rolls-Royce, Stutz seem reluctant to talk about power outputs.

Front engine, rear drive. V8, 5000 to 8200cc.
Max speed: 180km/h (112mph)
Length: 751cm (296in)
Weight: 2844kg (6270lb)

Aston Martin Lagonda (GB)

William Towns was responsible for the futuristic design of this car, and it was the first attempt by Aston Martin to move out of the sports/coupé slot in which it had achieved so much. The Lagonda is luxuriously equipped, with high quality finish, much of the build being by hand at AML's Newport Pagnell factory in England.

Max speed: 225km/h (140mph)
Length: 528cm (207in)
Weight: 2096kg (4622lb)

Hongki (CHI)

A luxury limousine produced in China, mainly for use by top officials so production is fairly limited. The V8, 5.7 litre engine drives the rear wheels and gives a staid performance. Styling is upright and conservative.

Max speed: 170km/h (106mph)
Length: 597cm (235in)
Weight: 2724kg (6006lb)

Cadillac Fleetwood 75 (USA)

This is the car for film stars and important politicians to ride about in. No one can overlook the impressive bulk of the Fleetwood as it draws up outside big hotels. Although the standard car has three rows of seats, and can carry eight people in comfort, there are those who need even more space. In that case the 5.4 metre (18ft) length can be extended by adding an extra centre section. Unusually for such a large car the V8 engine drives through the front wheels, chiefly to avoid having a hump in the floor caused by the transmission tunnel. As might be expected the standard of trim is very high: thick carpets and upholstery, tinted windows and air-conditioning are all standard equipment, and most of the limousines have television sets, hi-fi and even a bar in the rear compartment.

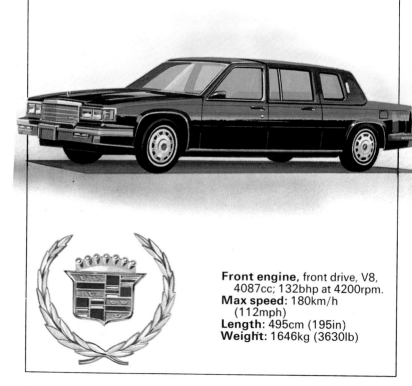

Front engine, front drive, V8, 4087cc; 132bhp at 4200rpm.
Max speed: 180km/h (112mph)
Length: 495cm (195in)
Weight: 1646kg (3630lb)

Compact/City Cars

Citroën AX

The smooth Citroën lines are continued with this new supermini, but the AX is far less complex than some of its bigger brothers. A new series of engines and gearboxes have been developed, and there is a sporting version on the way.

Max speed: 145km/h (90mph)
Length: 350cm (138in)
Weight: 641kg (1414lb)

Honda Civic J

Neat and unfussy lines for this compact three-door model, with headlamps flush against the sloping line of the bonnet. Options of 1.3 and 1.5 litre engines, both with belt-driven overhead camshaft and three valves per cylinder. There is also the choice of a five-speed manual gearbox or Honda's own three-speed automatic transmission. Reliability has become Honda's special hallmark.

Front engine, front drive. Four cylinders, 1342cc; 61bhp at 5500rpm.
Max speed: 154km/h (96mph)
Length: 381cm (150in)
Weight: 798kg (1760lb)

Trabant 601 (DDR)

A true motoring oddity, as the last two-stroke car still in production. Produced in the German Democratic Republic, the Trabant is only sold in Eastern bloc countries. A twin cylinder, 595cc engine drives the front wheels.

Max speed: 98km/h (61mph)
Length: 396cm (156in)
Weight: 613kg (1353lb)

Lancia Y10 (I)

Lancia returns to the small car market with the bob-tailed Y10. It is also seen in its native Italy with the Autobianchi badge. The smallest version uses the Fiat FIRE (Fully Integrated Robotized Engine) engine, while at the other end of the scale there is the 1.1 litre turbo. The unusual rear suspension uses an Omega-shaped centre pivoted beam, which Fiat have also adopted for the latest Panda model.

Front engine, front drive. Four cylinders, 999cc; 45bhp at 5000rpm to 1049cc turbo, 85bhp at 5750rpm.
Max speed: 145–180km/h (90–112mph).
Length: 340cm (134in)
Weight: 718kg (1584lb)

AUSTIN ROVER

Austin Mini Mayfair GB

This much-loved car was launched in August 1959 and is still going strong. Alec Issigonis's clever space-saving design placed the engine across the car, with the gearbox in the engine oil pan, driving the front wheels. The basic design has not changed much in all those years, still using the elderly but reliable 998cc A-plus engine which has its origins in the late 1940s. The suspension uses rubber cones, which give fantastic handling. During the 1960s the sporting 1293cc Mini-Cooper S's won the Monte Carlo Rally three times and it took a Porsche 911 to beat them. Despite being only 304cm (120in) long, there is still room for four adults and a reasonable amount of luggage. Early models suffered from all sorts of problems, including water leaks and flooded ignition, but over the years all have been solved. The Mayfair is the 'luxury' version, with smart upholstery and door trim.

Front engine, front drive. Four cylinders, 998cc; 41bhp at 5000rpm.
Max speed: 132km/h (82mph)
Length: 304cm (120in)
Weight: 596kg (1315lb)

Fiat Panda 45   (I)

A chunky and very practical little three-door hatchback, it uses the smallest of the FIRE engines developed jointly by Fiat and Peugeot. The robot-built FIRE engine has many fewer parts than some older designs. The latest version of the Panda has the 'Omega' rear suspension originally developed for the Lancia Y10; this uses a U-shaped beam, pivoted at the centre.

Max speed: 125km/h (78mph)
Length: 340cm (134in)
Weight: 698kg (1540lb)

Mazda/Ford Festiva   (J)

This is a real mixture of a car, with engines from Mazda, body a joint Ford/Mazda production – and the car built in South Korea. It was originally intended as a replacement for the West German-made Fiesta in 1979, but the project was dropped during the oil crisis. The Festiva is now being sold as a Ford in the USA and a Mazda elsewhere.

Five-speed gearbox.
Length: 347cm (137in)

Saloons

Mercedes-Benz 190E 2.3 16

This is the fastest of the small Mercedes-Benz 190 models, and an example of Anglo-German co-operation. The special cylinder head, with twin overhead camshafts and four valves per cylinder, was developed by Cosworth in Britain, the same firm which produced the V8, 3.0 litre Formula One engine and the Indy and CART winning derivatives. Output is 185bhp, which gives the car a top speed of around 225km/h (140mph). The suspension has been modified to handle the extra performance, with stiffer springs and ventilated disc brakes.

Front engine, rear drive. Four cylinders, 2299cc; 185bhp at 6200rpm.
Max speed: 225km/h (140mph)
Length: 441cm (174in)
Weight: 1257kg (2772lb)

D

Alfa Romeo 75 2.5 V6

An example of brilliant Italian engineering, with a 2.5 litre fuel injection V6 engine driving the rear wheels. Its layout is a little unusual, with the gearbox in unit with the final drive, which gives good weight distribution. The interior design is unconventional too, with roof-mounted switches and U-shaped handbrake lever.

Max speed: 209km/h (130mph)
Length: 431cm (170in)
Weight: 1157kg (2552lb)

Lancia Thema

This is Lancia's 'flagship' model, with the option of 2.0 litre turbo or ordinary, 2.8 litre V6 diesel engines. Some of the early development work was done with Saab of Sweden in what was called the Type 4 project. Saab's version is the 9000, and Fiat's the Croma. Front wheel drive gives a flat floor inside.

Max speed: 195km/h (121mph)
Length: 460cm (181in)
Weight: 1120kg (2470lb)

Audi 80 D

The new, low drag version of Audi's smallest model. Originally designed as a hatchback, it was later changed to a saloon. It has a simple but very effective safety system named Procon Ten, which pulls the steering column away from the driver in the event of a head-on accident. As well as the front drive versions, there is a four-wheel drive quattro model.

Max speed: 180km/h (112mph)
Length: 439cm (173in)
Weight: 1083kg (2389lb)

Peugeot 309 F

The big, curved rear window and small tail puts this French newcomer at the halfway point between being a hatchback and saloon. It fits in between the little 205 and the 406, launched in 1987. Recently a three-door version has been introduced, and a high performance 1.9 litre GTi model.

Max speed: 152km/h (95mph)
Length: 403cm (159in)
Weight: 858kg (1892lb)

Front engine, front
  drive. V6 2494cc;
  173bhp at 6000rpm.
Max speed: 207km/h
  (129mph)
Length: 485cm
  (191in)
Weight: 1328kg
  (2927lb)

Honda Legend   J

The Legend is Honda's version
of the joint design project between the Japanese company and
Rover in Britain. The 2.5 litre, V6
Honda engine drives the front
wheels, and the car is available
with a manual gearbox or four-
speed overdrive automatic transmission. There is a high standard
of equipment, with power steering, electric windows and air-
conditioning.

Nissan Bluebird   J

A classic three-box saloon which
Nissan is now assembling in a
new plant in Britain, to supply
European Common Market
countries. A transverse engine
drives the front wheels. Engine
options range from 1.6 to 2.0 litre
turbo, and diesel.

Max speed: 165km/h (103mph)
Length: 437cm (172in)
Weight: 1007kg (2222lb)

Holden Commodore

General Motors' 'down under' version of the Opel Commodore. At present the old body shape is being used, with the new Omega version appearing next year. The most powerful model uses a 5.0 litre, V8 engine, giving a top speed of 190km/h (118mph).

Max speed: 165km/h (103mph)
Length: 472cm (186in)
Weight: 1217kg (2684lb)

Toyota Crown (J)

A rare car outside Japan, as Toyota export few of these big saloons. Engines vary from a 2.0 to 3.0 litre, with 6 cylinders in line. Fastest of the Crowns is the supercharged 160bhp version, with a top speed of 209km/h (130mph).

Max speed: 160km/h (100mph)
Length: 470cm (185in)
Weight: 1267kg (2794lb)

Citroën 2CV

The Deux Chevaux has the distinction of being the oldest and one of the oddest cars still made. It was created 51 years ago, with the proviso that it must be able to carry a basket of eggs across a ploughed field without breaking one!

Max speed: 114km/h (71mph)
Length: 383cm (151in)
Weight: 583kg (1287lb)

BMW M5 **D**

At the other end of the spectrum from the 2CV, this BMW has a six-cylinder, 24-valve engine developed from the one originally used in the M1 sports coupé. The 5-Series body may look a little old-fashioned and upright, but under the bonnet the 3.5 litre engine produces a massive 286bhp. The suspension and brakes have been heavily uprated to handle the extra performance – this is a car which can get to 96.5km/h (60mph) in a little over six seconds and has a top speed of 244km/h (152mph).

Front engine, front drive. Six cylinders, 3453cc; 286bhp at 6500rpm.
Max speed: 244km/h (152mph)
Length: 459cm (181in)
Weight: 1427kg (3146lb)

Coupes

Audi Sport quattro 2 + 2

Audi produced the first high performance four-wheel drive car in 1980, when the original quattro was launched. The Sport is the uprated version of the standard quattro, with its turbocharged, five-cylinder 2.1 litre engine producing 306bhp. With its wide tyres, rally-bred suspension and of course, permanent four-wheel drive, the Sport quattro has incredible performance and outstanding handling.

Max speed: 249km/h (155mph)
Length: 416cm (164in)
Weight: 1297kg (2860lb)

Renault Alpine GTA V6 Turbo

This French-made coupé has rather unusual construction. A steel chassis carries the suspension and engine, while the bodywork is in plastic. The midmounted engine is the V6 which was developed jointly by Peugeot, Renault and Volvo. In its turbo injection form, it develops 200bhp. Suspension is independent all round, with massive disc brakes for stopping.

Mid engine, rear drive. V6, 2458cc; 200bhp at 7550rpm.
Max speed: 249km/h (155mph)
Length: 432cm (170in)
Weight: 1177kg (2596lb)

BMW 635CSi

This low, handsome BMW coupé featured in the European Touring Car Championship series. In its CSi form, the 6-Series has a deeper front air dam and boot top spoiler. The sporting suspension and handling exploits the 286bhp developed by the 3.5 litre, 24 valve engine, which drives the rear wheels.

Max speed: 254km/h (158mph)
Length: 492cm (194in)
Weight: 1496kg (3300lb)

Opel Manta GSi

Despite its age – it was launched in 1975 – the Manta is still a very popular model, with its straightforward front engine, rear drive layout. The six-cylinder, 2.4 litre, fuel injection engine has an unusual high mounted camshaft, right at the top of the cylinder block. The GSi has the Berlinetta rather than hatchback body.

Max speed: 215km/h (134mph)
Length: 444cm (175in)
Weight: 1092kg (2409lb)

Front engine, rear
drive. Four cylinders
2497cc; 220bhp at
5800rpm.
Max speed: 246km/h
(153mph)
Length: 424cm
(167in)
Weight: 1277kg
(2816lb)

Porsche 944 Turbo

Developed from the 924 model,
the latest version of the 944
Turbo has a new engine, with one
bank of four cylinders from the
V8 engine used in the 928. There
are now twin overhead camshafts, with four valves per cylinder. The front engine and
rear drive layout means that the
944 Turbo is very well balanced. Pop-up headlamps, and a
smooth front and rear wing all
add to the car's good aerodynamics.

Volvo 480ES (S)

An elegant newcomer to the
Volvo range, very different from
the rather conservative styling of
the big cars. The 1.7 litre engine is
based on a Renault unit, but is
built specially for Volvo, and
drives the front wheels. The
480ES has a practical hatchback
design.

Max speed: 189km/h (118mph)
Length: 426cm (168in)
Weight: 997kg (2200lb)

Aston Martin Zagato

I   **GB**

The small Italian coachbuilding firm Zagato and Aston Martin have collaborated before, in the 1960s, when they produced the elegant DB4GT, the car which appeared in the James Bond film *Goldfinger*. A meeting at a motor show between the heads of the new companies produced the idea that they should collaborate once more, and this is the result. Aston Martin supply the running chassis and engine, and Zagato adds the handmade bodywork, constructed from light alloy panels. These cars are really exclusive – only 50 of them were built and the price was high. But there was so much interest that all 50 were sold before the first car was completed. The powerplant is a tuned version of the Vantage V8, and because the chassis and body are lighter than the Vantage, the Zagato has a potential top speed of nearly 321km/h (200mph). The interior is also specially designed, but the shorter overall length means that the Zagato offers room for only two.

Front engine, rear drive. V8, 5341cc; 432bhp at 6250rpm.
Max speed: 299km/h (186mph)
Length: 439cm (173in)
Weight: 1646kg (3630lb)

Chevrolet Corvette (USA)

One of the classic American sports cars, it dates back to the 1960s. A feature of the Corvette has always been its anti-corrosion glass fibre and plastic bodywork, which is carried on a steel platform chassis. Last year a soft-top convertible version joined the two-door coupé model. The Corvette still features a big, 5.7 litre V8 engine, although the exhaust emission regulations have trimmed back its power a great deal when compared with the days when it rated as one of the real 'muscle cars'. Independent suspension is used with ventilated disc brakes on all four wheels. While the Corvette is still the slightly old-fashioned, long bonnet car, there are moves to push it sharp-ly forward against some of the more exotic imports such as Ferrari and Lamborghini. A hint of the new look Corvette could be contained in the Corvette Indy, a General Motors concept car produced with involvement from Lotus and featuring among other things a computer-controlled 'active suspension' system.

Front engine, rear drive. V8, 5733cc; 233bhp at 4000rpm.
Max speed: 230km/h (143mph)
Length: 447cm (176in)
Weight: 1461kg (3223lb)

Front engine, rear drive. Four cylinder, 2301cc; 147bhp at 4400rpm automatic transmission, 157bhp at 4600rpm manual gearbox.
Max speed: 189km/h (118mph)
Length: 502cm (198in)
Weight: 1437kg (3168lb)

USA

Ford Thunderbird Coupé Turbo

The T-Bird may have been slimmed down a lot since its launch, but it is still one of Ford's prestige models. The four cylinder, 2.3 litre turbo engine makes this version the fastest of the range of Thunderbirds. Transmission options offered are a five-speed manual gearbox or three-speed automatic. There is still a V8 version, using a 4.9 litre engine.

Pontiac Fiero GT USA

For a US manufacturer, the layout of the Fiero is unusual. Instead of using the conventional front engine, rear drive layout, this car has its six-cylinder transverse engine situated behind the seats. The rear wheels are driven through a four speed manual gearbox or automatic transmission. The body styling is sleek, and the GT has a prominent wing at the base of the rear window.

Max speed: 199.5km/h (124mph)
Length: 419cm (165in)
Weight: 1222kg (2695lb)

Isuzu Piazza (J)

This car is based on a model produced by Giugiaro in 1979, called Ace of Clubs. The Isuzu has smart, wedge-shaped styling, with semi-concealed headlamps. The choice of three engines includes a turbo injection version, driving the rear wheels.

Max speed: 168km/h (105mph)
Length: 439cm (173in)
Weight: 1157kg (2552lb)

Mitsubishi Starion Turbo (J)

This big 2 + 2 coupé has a hatchback, giving the Starion a useful amount of boot space with two people in the car. The front-mounted engines – 2.6 litre injection or 2.0 litre turbo – drive the rear wheels. An unusual feature is the attachment of the seat belts to the door, keeping them out of the way when rear passengers are getting in or out.

Max speed: 220km/h (137mph)
Length: 441cm (174in)
Weight: 1257kg (2772lb)

Subaru XT

Another example of the way in which the Japanese carmakers are moving into the coupé market. The striking XT embodies a number of unusual features, not least its part time four-wheel drive, taken from Subaru's other 4 × 4 model range. The car normally runs with the drive at the front, but in slippery conditions, where more traction is required, the driver can select full four-wheel drive. The flat 'boxer' engine, with turbocharger, is also unusual, and the electronically controlled air suspension automatically adjusts the height of the car.

Front engine, two- or four-wheel drive. Flat four cylinders, 1782cc; 113bhp at 4800rpm.
Max speed: 199.5km/h (124mph)
Length: 444cm (175in)
Weight: 1127kg (2486lb)

Toyota MR2

The mid-engine layout of this two-seater car has turned out to be very popular. The MR2 has brilliant performance and wonderful handling and is a real sports car. The twin overhead camshaft, four valve per cylinder engine is the same as that used in the front wheel drive Celica GT. The smooth, sloping nose, with pop-up headlamps and the prominent rear spoiler make the MR2 look very sporty. More recent variants of the MR2 go for even better performance from the little car with the fitment of a supercharger to the engine. Complaints that the sunroof did not let in enough air have been met by the production of a model in which the two roof panels lift out, leaving only a T-shaped reinforcement. The mid-engine layout means that the car has luggage space at both front and rear.

Mid engine, rear wheel drive. Four cylinders, 1587cc; 115bhp at 6600rpm.
Max speed: 199.5km/h (124mph)
Length: 393cm (155in)
Weight: 1037kg (2288lb)

Ford Mustang SVO USA

The Mustang sports car quickly became a legend in American automobile history. But while the early cars were well received as true sports cars, later models were criticised for looking ordinary and performing badly. Ford's answer to its critics was to ask its Special Vehicles Operations to breathe some fire into the Mustang, and this is the result. It has a top speed of more than 193km/h (120mph), a sporty manual gearbox and revised suspension settings to cope with the extra power. Disc brakes are fitted on all four wheels. The engine has an air-to-air intercooler and electronic fuel injection.

Max speed: 199.5km/h (124mph)
Length: 459cm (181in)
Weight: 1412kg (3113lb)

Hatchbacks

Austin Maestro

This hatchback slots in between the Metro 'supermini' and the saloon and estate Montego. The smallest engine is the 1275cc A-Plus, while the most powerful is the 2.0 lître injection MG version.

Max speed: 156km/h (97mph)
Length: 401cm (158in)
Weight: 875kg (1930lb)

Citroën BX

The first new model to come from one of the world's most unconventional carmakers. The BX was styled by the great Italian Bertone and retains a number of special Citroën features including the clever pneumatic suspension which allows the car to ride on air. The bonnet and tailgate are both moulded in plastic which helps keep the weight down.

Max speed: 165 km/h (109mph)
Length: 423cm (166in)
Weight: 950 kg (2095lb)

Ford Sierra **GB**

Ford of Europe's aerodynamic three box hatchback has variants ranging from the most basic 1.3 litre version up to the 241km/h (150mph) 2.0 litre turbocharged RS Cosworth. Ford opted for a simple front engine, rear drive layout for ease of servicing. The exception is the four wheel drive version with the 2.9 litre, V6 engine, made in hatchback as well as station wagon form. The standard three-door version has been extensively revised for release in 1987, with a larger glass area, and a neater nose *(see below)*.

Front engine, rear drive. Four cylinder, 1597cc; 75bhp at 4900rpm.
Max speed: 151km/h (94mph)
Length: 439cm (173in)
Weight: 990kg (2183lb)

Vauxhall Cavalier (GB)

This is the British-made version of the West German Opel Ascona, available in both four-door sedan and five-door hatchback form. The 2.0 litre engine is new, designed to comply with the proposed European exhaust emission regulations which come into effect in 1989. The engine is the biggest version of the 'Family 2' single overhead camshaft power unit.

Front engine, front drive. Four cylinders, 1598cc; 75bhp at 5600rpm.
Max speed: 187km/h (116mph)
Length: 437cm (171in)
Weight: 1010kg (2271lb)

Opel Corsa **D**

General Motors built a brand new factory in Spain to produce the Corsa, which is also known as the Nova in its British, right-hand drive form. There are three engine options in the front drive saloon, from 1.0 to 1.3 litres. The three-box body is made in two- and four-door form, to provide an alternative to the hatchback.

Max speed: 143km/h (89mph)
Length: 363cm (143in)
Weight: 738kg (1628lb)

VW Polo *(left)* **D**

The station wagon look of the VW Polo has set a new style for small hatchback cars, where the aim is to get the maximum amount of space inside, while keeping the outside dimensions small. A number of different variations have been tried, including a coupé model with a slanted rear roof. The fastest Polo is the car fitted with Volkswagen's interesting spiral super-charger system, allowing the little car to challenge the Porsche on Germany's unlimited speed *autobahnen.* The CL uses the smallest of three engine sizes available. Production of the Polo has switched almost completely to Spain, where VW has recently taken over the Seat company and its production plants.

Front engine, front drive. Four
    cylinders, 1043cc; 45bhp at
    5600rpm.
Max speed: 141km/h (88mph)
Length: 365cm (144in)
Weight: 728kg (1606lb)

115

Fiat Uno

The Uno won the coveted European Car of the Year Award for Fiat who turned to master designer Giorgio Giugiaro to produce a new compact small car to replace the highly successful Fiat 127 hatchback. In the first four years of its life more than two million Unos have been built in a number of versions. The fastest model is the turbo, with a top speed in excess of 193km/h (120mph). There is also a diesel model which is popular in parts of Europe, including Italy, where diesel fuel is cheaper than petrol. The smallest is the FIRE engined model, so called because of the way the engine is built at a special factory run by robots. FIRE stands for Fully Integrated Robotized Engine.

Front engine, front drive. Four cylinders, 999cc; 45bhp at 5000rpm.
Max speed: 144km/h (90mph)
Length: 365cm (144in)
Weight: 1107kg (2442lb)

Seat Ibiza

When Seat planned the Ibiza, they chose Europe's best designers. Ital Design produced the snub-tailed body, while Porsche Design developed the single overhead camshaft engine. Much of the suspension is ex-Fiat Ritmo, which Seat used to build under licence from Fiat.

Max speed: 154km/h (96mph)
Length: 363cm (143in)
Weight: 898kg (1980lb)

Volvo 360GLT

The smaller 300-series Volvos use Renault-based engines, but this sporting hatchback has Volvo's own low friction and fuel efficient 2.0 litre fuel injection unit. An unusual feature is that the five-speed gearbox is not alongside the engine as normal, but at the back, in front of the rear axle. This has the advantage of moving weight to the back of the car, making it better balanced and therefore more stable. You can distinguish this high performance small Volvo from the rest of the range by the small spoiler fitted to the tailgate.

Front engine, rear drive. Four cylinders, 1986cc; 115bhp at 5700rpm.
Max speed: 185km/h (115mph)
Length: 431cm (170in)
Weight: 1087kg (2398lb)

Fiat Croma ⓘ

This is Fiat's version of the 'Type 4' model which was originally conceived jointly by Saab of Sweden and Lancia (which is now part of Fiat). The Croma is Fiat's first big front wheel drive car, replacing the unsuccessful rear drive 132/Argenta. Engine sizes range from 1.6 litre to the 2.0 litre carburettor and injection version, but the fastest of the Cromas is the 155bhp turbo model. There are also standard and turbo diesel models. Few Italian drivers bother with automatic transmission, but it can be had as an option on the 2.0 litre models. Under the skin these Type 4 models have many common parts.

Max speed: 170km/h (106mph)
Length: 449cm (177in)
Weight: 1095kg (2416lb)

FSO Polonez LE ⓅⓁ

In 1968 the Polish state motor company, FSO produced its first big model, the 125P. The Poles had accepted the Fiat 125 design right down to the engine and gearbox, in the same way that the 124 model had been used in the Soviet Union where Fiat had set up the Lada plant. Then in 1978 the Poles designed the Polonez hatchback without any outside help. However, the 125P floorplan, power train and suspension continues to be used.

Max speed: 154km/h (96mph)
Length: 427cm (168in)
Weight: 1122kg (2475lb)

Saab 9000

The 9000 was produced out of a combined development project between the Swedish Saab company and Lancia of Italy. The original idea was that the 9000 and the Lancia Thema should use many of the same parts. In the end the cars share only six minor body pressings, but the co-operation saved a lot of development time. The 9000 comes with a 2.0 litre turbo, or 2.0 litre fuel injection engine. A special electronic management system allows the car to run on even the cheapest and lowest grade fuel without damage to the engine. Saab has drawn extensively upon its experience as an aircraft builder for the design of the interior, which closely resembles the cockpit of an aircraft. The high standard of fittings includes heated seats for the front passengers. Top of the range models are fitted with anti-lock brakes.

Front engine, front drive. Four cylinders, 1985cc; 130bhp at 5300rpm.
Max speed: 190km/h (118mph)
Length: 462cm (182in)
Weight: 1297kg (2860lb)

Hyundai Pony GLS

The giant Hyundai corporation has been assembling cars mainly European Ford models, for a long time and South Korea's motor industry is booming. The Pony's body originally had five doors and was designed by the Italian stylist, Giugiaro. Now there is also a three-door model. The engine, gearboxes and suspension are all made under licence from Mitsubishi in Japan.

Max speed: 159km/h (99mph)
Length: 396cm (156in)
Weight: 868kg (1914lb)

Toyota Corolla GL *(right)* **J**

The Corolla shows most clearly how far the Japanese have come as carmakers, because the world's biggest selling car is not a Volkswagen or a Ford, it is the Toyota Corolla. One reason for its success is that the car does not attempt to blaze any new design trails. It is simple, well equipped and built to high standards to ensure reliability. There are several models available in addition to the hatchback, and they include estate, station wagon and saloon versions, and a liftback model which is essentially a coupé. The GL shown here uses the smallest engine available, the 1.3 litre unit which has three valves per cylinder (two instead of one inlet valve) to provide better economy and also less polluting exhaust emissions. Two manual gearboxes and four- and five-speeds are available as well as a three-speed automatic. Hatchback buyers can choose either three- or five-door body styles.

Front engine, front drive. Four cylinders, 1296cc; 81bhp at 6000rpm.
Max speed: 159km/h (99mph)
Length: 414cm (163in)
Weight: 873kg (1925lb)

Suzuki Cultus/Swift

Originally designed for General Motors in the USA, import restrictions meant that Suzuki had to look elsewhere for markets. The 1.0 litre version is made with three or four cylinders, while the 1.3 is four cylinders only, with four valves per cylinder.

Max speed: 170km/h (106mph)
Length: 358cm (141in)
Weight: 668kg (1474lb)

Trucks

▲ **The Swedish Vabis of 1902.** The driver and load were both completely unprotected, but the truck could carry 1.5 tonnes with reliability.

Early History

With the invention of the wheel it is certain that those early discoverers did not immediately think of making a passenger vehicle for themselves. Their first objective was to take some of the burden from their shoulders and to be able to shift heavy weights, without breaking their backs. This was the first truck. Even today it is true that in those less well-developed countries which are only now switching from animal-drawn to motorized transportation the first demand is always for a load carrier.

The modern truck owes much of its development to the motor car, and there are as a result many parallels between the two histories.

◀ **A Canadian** logging truck.

▲ By 1921 vans like this Ford TT were
a common sight on the roads.

Like the early cars the first real trucks relied on steam power, because
at the time most people believed that was where the future lay for
motorized transport. The first designs by the steam vehicle pioneers
Cugnot and Trevithick are described earlier (*page 13*). Like the motor
car there are differing opinions as to who produced the first truck, but
it seems that Henry Ford is the prime candidate for that honour.

Ford is credited with selling a panel side delivery truck to a shoe
company in Detroit in 1899. This was quite a feat because most
businesses would not trust the delivery of their products to the new-
fangled internal combustion engine. Added to this was the consideration that most of them had large stables of horses and the staff to run
them. Henry Ford countered this with a special advertising slogan for
his Ford Model T pick-up which proclaimed: 'It doesn't need feeding
when standing still'. His claim for economy was quite accurate.
Figures from those early days show that a Model T cost about half the
amount needed to maintain a horse and cart.

Even so, pioneers like Ford found it difficult to convince people,
and especially the American government which was strongly commit-
ted to support the building of railway lines across its vast country. But
it was the size of the USA which was to help the truck business come
into its own. America, with its wide open spaces and enormous

▶ **A Humber** utility vehicle used in the Second World War.

variations in terrain and climate, was the ideal testing ground for developing truck technology, although the early engineers paid little heed to the basic design requirements essential to the modern carrier.

To be used commercially the truck had to be reliable, and it had to be capable of carrying heavy weights. The car designers might have got away with a few errors when considering the difficulties of carrying four people, but truck loads caused major problems with steering, suspension and the design of the chassis. However, just as two world wars speeded up the development of the aeroplane, so they accelerated the production of trucks. Horse-drawn transport was rapidly replaced by motor vehicles in the First World War (1914–1918), and because of the number of vehicles required, it became

▼ **Fiat Type 15 trucks** and Type 2 cars lined up for the British Army in 1917.

▲ These two Mack Ultra-liners
illustrate the difference between
'bonneted' (*right hand side*)
and 'cab-over' designs.

worthwhile to develop the design of trucks, and the quality of fuel and tyres. At the end of the war a large number of redundant military vehicles were put to civilian use, increasing the amount of traffic on the roads enormously.

Meanwhile just as experiments were made with electric cars, so different possibilities were being explored in the truck world too. Electric vans had large storage batteries, and were built to be used for carrying lightweight loads in towns and cities. But it was found that the jolting of the vehicle over poorly surfaced streets, on the solid tyres then in use, badly damaged the battery. Another alternative, which was and still is more widely used in Europe than the USA, is diesel, a more economical fuel than petrol.

Truck Design

Overall design of trucks has changed dramatically over the years, especially the layout of the driver's cab and the engine. Early trucks positioned the engine inside the cab beside the driver, later designs opted for a conventional bonnet or had the engine under the floor.

But the most important feature of any truck is the amount of cargo it can carry – truck operators call this the 'payload potential'. A few operators add to this the need to have the largest area possible. These operators would like to be able to use the biggest vehicles they could make, but such huge trucks would quickly destroy roads and bridges, and cause havoc with other traffic. There are therefore specific limits on weights and lengths of trucks. They vary from country to country, but larger places such as America and Australia can afford to run bigger trucks than those which are generally used in Europe. At the other end of the scale the tiny Channel Island of Guernsey has to have its trucks specially built, because the roads are so narrow.

Modern trucks can be divided into two main categories by their construction – rigid or articulated. The rigid truck has one straight chassis frame with the engine at the front, and up to four axles. The articulated truck comes in two parts, a 'tractor' unit which carries the

◀ This picture of a Canadian lumber truck shows how, by 'articulating', a long truck can negotiate a corner more easily.

▶ This Steyr tipper is a rigid truck, with one straight chassis frame.

engine, the cab and the driving wheels, and a trailer which is coupled up to the tractor section by a special connector which allows the rig to 'bend' or 'articulate' in the middle. The advantage of this is that the cab section can be turned almost at right angles to the trailer and therefore the whole combination can turn in a much tighter circle than a rigid truck. Having a detachable load is useful too. If an operator wants to ship overseas he can load the trailer only, saving space on the boat and keeping his tractor on the side of the water where it earns its keep, while the load travels across to be picked up by another tractor when it arrives.

▲ **A Mercedes-Benz** drawbar combination, which allows even greater flexibility when cornering.

Articulated trucks are usually limited to 12.2 metres (40ft) in length and the rigid chassis maximum is even less, 9 metres (30ft). A longer combination uses a trailer with a drawbar, fixed to the back of a long rigid truck, rather like a caravan to a car. In Europe the most up-to-date designs feature a special drawbar which automatically adjusts the distance between the two units for better cornering. When going straight it closes the gap, reducing the overall length and allowing the operator to have more loadspace. In Europe these combinations can often be up to 18 metres (59ft) long, so other drivers had better take notice of the 'long vehicle' sign when they see it. In America even longer combinations are permitted with an articulated truck attached to a trailer. These are called 'double-bottoms'. To cross the vast distances across the outback in Australia four or five trailers linked up to one tractor are used, known as 'roadtrains'.

Besides the payload potential, the other item of most interest to the commercial vehicle operator is how much it will cost to make the delivery. The huge engines on the modern truck with intercooled

LONG-DISTANCE TRUCKS

In many parts of the world trucks hauling huge loads are the most economical method of transporting cargo over vast distances. In areas such as America, Australia and the Middle East, trucks are the vital link with remote regions where there are so few people that it is not worth building a railway. Sometimes these journeys are fraught with difficulties. In Canada and Alaska temperatures as low as −40°C can freeze diesel fuel, so the fuel tanks have to be heated, and drivers often leave their engines running all the time.

In Europe many long-distance trucks carry plates with the initials TIR, standing for *Transports Internationaux Routiers*. This shows customs officers that the load has been sealed up and cleared for an international run, so that they do not have to check it. Most TIR trucks use special purpose-built trailers that can be completely sealed before being given their TIR plates. In Australia road trains often drive along dirt tracks because they are too large to drive along the public highways. They are fitted with special tyres, and can travel at up to 90km/h (55mph).

A Californian long-distance truck.

129

turbo diesels can consume large amounts of fuel. Heavier weights need more powerful engines, and in order to avoid problems which might arise if the operator overloaded trucks fitted with puny engines, most countries have a code which sets out the amount of load which can be carried by a certain size of engine. This is usually calculated at about six brake horse power for each metric tonne carried, so a 38-tonne truck needs to have an engine capable of producing a minimum 228bhp.

Today's engines are much more efficient than they used to be: careful design has made them use less fuel and produce more power. Turbochargers are a comparatively new innovation on cars, but they have been used in trucks for years. A turbo harnesses the power of the fast moving gases from the exhaust to drive a turbine, like a millwheel, which compresses the mixture of fuel and air that goes into the engine. By squeezing it up, more mixture is pushed into the engine, so that when it is ignited there is a bigger explosion, and the engine produces more power. Trucks also use intercoolers. They work with the turbo and do as their name suggests, cool down the charge of mixture, reducing its volume, so that even more fuel and air can be crammed into the cylinder.

▼ 1980s cab refinement is
exemplified here by Volvo's new FL7/10
cab.

▲ **One of the tests** to satisfy
Sweden's rigorous safety requirements.

Cab Comfort

Barely 20 years ago most truck cabs were poorly constructed with very little thought for the comfort or health of the driver. Engines generated what would today be regarded as quite unacceptable levels of heat, noise and vibration. In recent years manufacturers have tried to make the driver's job less demanding physically by improving the layout of the controls inside the cab, sound insulation, cab suspension and making access to the cab easier. Cabs are built to be more comfortable, and safer. Spacious sleeper accommodation for drivers who are away from home for days at a time is also important. In the USA, where journeys can often take weeks rather than days, this accommodation may include running water, and a bathroom, kitchen and dining area. This saves on motel bills. It is not unlikely that such trucks will be driven by a husband and wife team, travelling and working together.

With so many journeys now being undertaken by European as well as American drivers, there has been some concern that drivers might spend too long at the wheel. To avoid this problem a device called a 'tachograph' is fitted in the cab. This looks a bit like a speedometer into which a circular card is fitted. The card makes a record of what happens to the truck, how fast it goes and how long it stops, so that drivers are not tempted to cheat and miss their breaks. It is fair to say that drivers don't like these devices: they call the tachographs 'the spy in the cab', but all trucks and coaches in Europe now have to carry them by law.

As commercial vehicle technology unfolds towards the year 2000, futuristic developments come closer to reality. A number of experimental trucks have been built using lighter but expensive materials such as carbon-fibre for propeller shafts, refined glass-fibre for leaf

▼ **This picture shows** the circular card being inserted into a tachograph, now carried by all trucks and coaches.

▲ Leyland's TX450 concept truck,
which is being used to test a host of
'space age' technical developments.

springs, and alloy spaceframes for chassis structures. It seems certain
that air suspension will become more widely adopted, giving a
smoother ride. On-board computers are set to revolutionize commercial operation. The computer will deal with much of the paperwork as
well as planning delivery routes and monitoring the condition of the
vehicle.

Rigid, 2 Axles, 1 Driven

Mercedes-Benz 814 (D)

Built by Mercedes-Benz, the world's largest producer of trucks of over 6 tonnes gvw, the 814 is the most popular model in the refined LN2 range introduced in 1985.

Engine: Mercedes OM 366 5.9 litre, 6-cylinder diesel, 134bhp.
Gearbox: Mercedes G3 5-speed synchromesh.
Gvw: 7.5 tonnes.

DAF FA 1100 (NL)

Though a leading exporter of heavy chassis DAF sells its middleweight models, like the FA 1100, mainly in the Netherlands. Its cab was developed by four European manufacturers.

Engine: DAF DT615 6.2 litre, 6-cylinder turbocharged diesel, 158bhp.
Gearbox: 5-speed synchromesh.
Gvw: 9.7 tonnes.

Dennis Delta 1600 GB

In recent years the Dennis company has dealt mainly with the municipal market: building refuse collectors and fire appliances. The Delta is the company's only general goods-carrying chassis, and its specification is very conventional.

Engine: Perkins T6.354, 5.8 litre, 6-cylinder turbocharged diesel, 155bhp.
Gearbox: 6-speed overdrive synchromesh.
Gvw: 16.25 tonnes.

Mitsubishi Fuso FM J

Known better in Europe for its passenger cars, Mitsubishi is nevertheless one of Japan's major truck producers, as well as being one of the leading shipbuilding and heavy engineering corporations. The FM chassis is at the lighter end of the Fuso range of trucks. Various innovations have updated this range, including a more modern and refined cab, and engine turbocharging, which improves efficiency. The cab has also received some attention, with new electronic technology making controls light to use, and generally more comfort and convenience for the driver.

Engine: Mitsubishi 6D-14, 6.6 litre, 6-cylinder diesel, 154bhp.
Gearbox: 5/6/10-speed synchromesh.
Brakes: Vacuum-assisted hydraulic
Gvw: 14 tonnes.

Engine: MAN 5.7 litre,
6-cylinder diesel,
136bhp.
Gearbox: 5-speed
synchromesh.
Brakes: Air-assisted
hydraulic.
Gvw: 7.5 tonnes.

MAN-VW 8.136

In the mid '70s MAN of Munich entered into collaboration with Volkswagenswerk. MAN already specialized in the production of heavy trucks but wanted to develop middleweight trucks to bridge a gap in their output. The 8.136 is the biggest-selling model from the resulting MT range, and it shares the cab of the VW LT.

Engine: Fiat 2.5 litre,
4-cylinder direct
injection
turbocharged diesel,
92bhp.
Gearbox: 5-speed
synchromesh.
Gvw: 3.5 tonnes.

Iveco Turbo Daily 35.10

Iveco introduced direct-injection in small capacity diesel engines when the Turbo Daily was launched in 1985. Unlike its competitor from Ford, the Iveco engine is also turbocharged, giving better fuel economy and smoother running. It is available either as a complete van, or as a chassis-cab on which bodies can be mounted. The Daily is noted for its spacious and well-designed cab.

Iveco 175.17

Fiat's truck-building subsidiary, Iveco, has one of the largest output and sales in Europe. In the UK the company has joined forces with Ford in a joint research, manufacturing and marketing exercise. The latest 16-tonne truck retains its spacious cab but gives better and more economical performance than before.

Engine: Iveco 5.9 litre, 6-cylinder turbocharged, 177bhp.
Gearbox: ZF 6-speed synchromesh.
Gvw: 17 tonnes.

Renault G170

The G170 cab readily identified as having its origins in the 1970s project in which Saviem (now part of Renault) was a partner. It is one of the many G range middle to heavyweight Renaults. At 16.25 tonnes it is in the weight range which has been made popular because of legislation.

Engine: Renault 5.5 litre 6-cylinder turbo-intercooled diesel, 169bhp.
Gearbox: 5/10-speed synchromesh.
Gvw: 16.25 tonnes.

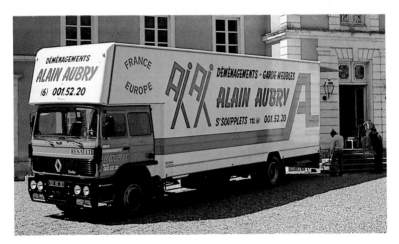

137

Hino FF J

Japan's biggest manufacturer and exporter of middleweight and heavy trucks, Hino is nevertheless a relatively new name, dating only from 1947. The FF is a popular 13-tonne truck of orthodox specification – part of a range of rigid 4 by 2's.

Engine: Hino 6.44 litre, 6-cylinder diesel, 165bhp.
Gearbox: 6-speed synchromesh.
Gvw: 13 tonnes.

ERF E6 GB

In 1986 ERF, the last privately-owned British truck manufacturer, completely revised its range of heavy trucks, from 16.25 tonnes upwards. Known in its updated form as the E-series, it features a more spacious and modern cab. The E6 is a 16-tonne rigid powered by Cummins' latest 6BTA diesel engine.

Engine: Cummins 6BTA 5.9 litre, turbo-intercooled diesel, 180bhp.
Gearbox: Eaton 6-speed synchromesh.
Gvw: 16.25 tonnes.

Ford Cargo  **GB**

Introduced in 1981 as a successor to the popular D-series, Ford's Cargo rigid 4 by 2 models span a weight range from 6 to 16.25 tonnes. The modern cab has large glass areas including kerb-sighting windows low down in the doors.

Engine: Ford 4/6/6.2 litre, 4/6-cylinder diesels, up to 150bhp.
Gearbox: Ford 4/6/8-speed, or ZF 5-speed.
Gvw: 6 to 16.25 tonnes.

Leyland Roadrunner

Built for the UK market, the Roadrunner was introduced by Leyland in 1984. In 1986 it was updated with a new engine based on the Cummins 6BT engine. The Roadrunner has now been introduced in Europe, marketed by the Dutch DAF company under its own name. This DAF version doesn't feature the unusual kerb-sighting window in the cab door.

Engine: Cummins 6BT 5.9 litre, 6-cylinder diesel, 110/130bhp.
Gearbox: 5-speed Spicer synchromesh.
Brakes: Disc front, drum rear, air-hydraulic.
Gvw: 7.5 tonnes.

GB

Ford F600 USA

Typical of American middle-weight trucks, the F600 from Ford's Louisville range has bonneted styling and like many American trucks it is powered by a petrol rather than a diesel engine. There are many different versions listed, as well as numerous types of cab trim, ranging from the austere to the luxurious.

Engine: Ford 6.1 litre, V8 petrol, 174bhp.
Gearbox: New Process synchromesh.
Brakes: Power hydraulic with vacuum-hydraulic option.

Engine: GAZ 6.2 litre, 6-cylinder air-cooled diesel, 125bhp.
Gearbox: 5-speed synchromesh.

GAZ-66 SU

Diesel power is still a novelty in middleweight Russian trucks like this 4 tonne payload GAZ. The 6.2 litre GAZ engine is air-cooled, like those built in Czechoslovakia by Tatra and by Deutz in W. Germany. The rear axle can be used for hauling a drawbar both on and off surfaced roads.

140

Paccar BRA

Though marketed by Paccar in the USA and Canada under the Kenworth and Peterbilt marque names, the company's newest and lightest models are built in South America by Volkswagen of Brazil.

Engine: Cummins 8.3 litre, 6-cylinder turbocharged diesel, 210bhp.
Gearbox: Eaton 6-speed synchromesh.
Gvw: Up to 15 tonnes.

Engine: Pegaso 10.2 litre, 6-cylinder diesel.
Gearbox: ZF 6-speed synchromesh.
Cab: 'Techno' steel cab.

Isuzu FSR J

Isuzu claims to be Japan's longest-established truck builder, though since 1971 General Motors has held a significant financial stake. The FSR competes directly with Hino's FF models.

Engine: Isuzu 5.8 litre, 6-cylinder diesel, 150bhp.
Gearbox: 5/6-speed synchromesh.
Gvw: 9 tonnes.

Pegaso 1217 E

Enasa, which builds Pegaso trucks, is now the only Spanish heavy truck manufacturer. Subsidiaries include Seddon-Atkinson in the UK, and the company is collaborating with DAF on cab development. The 1217 is an extra heavy-duty four-wheeler which can operate with weights of up to 20 tonnes gross.

141

Engine: Renault 12
litre, 6-cylinder
turbo-intercooled
diesel, 331bhp.
Gearbox: Renault 18-
speed synchromesh.
Gvw: 19 tonnes.

Renault R340

At the top of Renault's heavy truck range are the 38-tonne payload models. The origins of their engine and cab engineering lie in the former Berliet marque.

The R340 has evolved as a more powerful version of the R310, popular in France. At the top of its range it carries the name Turboliner.

Scania P82

No trucks below 16.25 tonnes are built by Scania. The P82 is now powered by the Swedish company's new 8.5 litre lightly-turbocharged engine. For towing with a drawbar a more powerful variant, designated P92, is listed. The cab is un-usually spacious for this size of truck.

Engine: Scania 8.5 litre, 6-cylinder turbocharged diesel, 204bhp.
Gearbox: 5/10-speed synchromesh.
Gvw: 16.25 tonnes.

Volvo FL6

In its heaviest-duty form the FL6 is a 16.25 tonne truck, but lighter variants are also listed. New in 1985, the FL6 cab sits low on the chassis, making access easy for the driver and the cab more comfortable generally. However one penalty of the cab's low build is that the engine lies between the seats, making it difficult for the driver to cross the cab to the kerb side when making deliveries in busy city streets. Particular emphasis has been placed by Volvo on safety matters. The large windows allow a good field of view all round. The steel cab shell is tested by a swinging weight to conform to the rigorous Swedish strength requirements.

Engine: Volvo 5.5 litre, 6-cylinder turbocharged diesel 180bhp or turbocharged intercooled diesel, 207bhp.

Gearbox: ZF 5/6-speed, Volvo 8-speed synchromesh, or Allison fully-automatic.

Gvw: 12 to 16.25 tonnes.

143

Rigid, 2 Axles, Both Driven

Hino NZ J

The NZ is the only model in Hino's range of trucks to have a bonneted layout and 4 by 4 drive.

Engine: Hino 9.4 litre, 6-cylinder diesel, 215bhp (158kW).
Gearbox: 6-speed synchromesh.
Gvw: 14.3 to 16 tonnes.

Mercedes-Benz 1617-CAK D

During the mid '70s, Mercedes broke with tradition by adopting a forward-control (cab-over) design for nearly all its heavy trucks. Even those designed for off-road working where a bonneted layout had become taken for granted were changed. The 1617-CAK is an example of the new breed of cab-over Mercedes with all-wheel drive intended for use as a tipper.

Engine: Mercedes-Benz 5.9 litre, 6-cylinder turbocharged diesel, 169bhp.
Gearbox: 5-speed synchromesh.
Gvw: 16.2 tonnes.

144

Sisu SL 170-VK (SF)

Sisu is Finland's only heavy truck builder. Its heaviest models are powered by 14 litre Cummins diesels from the UK. The SL 170-VK is a bonneted 4 by 4 heavy-duty tipper/dumptruck.

Engine: Valmet 6.5 litre, 6-cylinder turbocharged diesel, 215bhp.
Gearbox: ZF S6–90 6-speed synchromesh.
Gvw: 20 tonnes.

Mercedes-Benz 1936 AK (D)

In the mid '70s Mercedes stopped producing bonneted heavy trucks, even for rugged off-road working. The 1936 AK competes in the 4 by 4 heavy market ,with MAN, Volvo and Scania vehicles.

Engine: Mercedes 18 litre V10 diesel, 360bhp.
Gearbox: ZF 16-speed synchromesh.
Gvw: 19 tonnes.

Rigid, 3 Axles, 2 Driven

Ginaf

This specialist Dutch truck manufacturer builds trucks which meet requirements not catered for by larger companies. In particular Ginaf builds trucks which can carry heavier weights than those normally permitted on the public roads. The picture shows a five-axled truck from the Ginaf range.

Engine: To customer's choice, often DAF 11.6 litre, turbocharged diesel.
Gearbox: ZF manual or automatic.
Gvw: 24.2 tonnes.

Scania P92 **S**

Most three-axled trucks from Scania, even those built to work both on and off the road have just one driven axle. But the P92 is built for foreign markets as a 6 by 4 vehicle. The bogie suspension is unusual for a continental or Scandinavian chassis in having four springs.

Engine: Scania 8.5 litre, 6-cylinder turbocharged diesel, 220bhp.
Gearbox: Scania 10-speed.
Gvw: 24.4 tonnes.

Engine: Cummins 14 litre, 6-cylinder turbocharged diesel, 290bhp.
Gearbox: Fuller 9-speed or Spicer 10-speed.
Gvw: 16.25 tonnes.

Bedford TM GB

Production of Bedford trucks for the commercial market is being phased out, and they will soon be built solely for military duties. The TM heavy range, launched in 1974, was designed around Detroit Diesel V6 and V8 two-stroke engines, but later examples have used Cummins 14 and 10 litre engines.

Engine: Caterpillar 14.6 litre, 6-cylinder turbocharged diesel, 325bhp.
Gearbox: Fuller 10-speed constant mesh.
Gvw: 32 tonnes.

Autocar DC USA

Autocar is a subsidiary of the White Trucks concern which is now owned by Volvo of Sweden. Volvo took over in 1983, but Autocar's products have changed very little, and still look very American to European eyes. Most Autocar chassis are custom-built class 8 (heavy-duty) models, with a bonneted layout as in the picture. The established DC-series has a steel, largely flat-panelled cab, and is built for rugged terrain.

Tatra T815 S.3 (CS)

Tatra was established as a truck builder before the turn of the century, though the name was not adopted till 1919. For many years the design 'trade mark' of Tatra vehicles has been their central-spine chassis, from which the wheels are suspended independently on swing axles which pivot around a longitudinal hinge. This gives a smooth ride over poor surfaces. All-wheel driven and rear-wheel driven six- and eight-wheelers are available.

Engine: Tatra 15.8 litre air-cooled V10 diesel 279bhp.
Gearbox: 5-speed contant mesh.
Gvw: 22 tonnes.

Kenworth C510 (USA)

From the Paccar range of extra-heavy duty trucks for work on and off the road, the bonneted C510 is sold in 6 by 6 as well as 6 by 4 form. Choice of rear suspension includes a design which combines the ruggedness of leaf springs with a very comfortable ride.

Engine: Cummins 10 litre, 6-cylinder turbocharged diesel, 240bhp
Gearbox: Eaton-Fuller 9-speed constant mesh.
Gvw: Up to 40 tonnes.

148

Leyland Landtrain GB

The Third World, and particularly Africa, is the main market for Leyland's heavy and rugged Landtrain range. Launched in 1980, it replaced the British state-owned company's old Super Hippo models. Cummins engines were selected for the Landtrain largely because of their proven durability. They also have a worldwide service network, although the injector fuel system used in these engines requires less servicing than the more common jerk-pump type.

Engine: Cummins 14 litre, 6-cylinder turbocharged diesel, 290bhp
Gearbox: Fuller 9-speed constant mesh.
Gvw: Up to 30 tonnes.

Dodge Commando 2 GB

A 6 by 4 truck intended mainly for tipper duties, the Commando carries the designation G24 and is powered by Perkins' V8.540 diesel. The cab and general chassis layout are similar to that of the two-axled Commandoes.

Engine: Perkins 8.8 litre, V8 diesel, 170bhp, turbocharged 230bhp.
Gearbox: Fuller 9-speed constant mesh.

Seddon-Atkinson 3–11 GB

Seddon Atkinson is a subsidiary of the Spanish state-owned Enasa group. The company's rigid 6 by 4's are popular because of their mechanical simplicity and low weight. The 3–11 is a new version of the 301 chassis.

Engine: Cummins 10 litre, 6-cylinder turbocharged diesel, 240bhp.
Gearbox: Fuller 9-speed constant mesh.

Rigid, 3 Axles, All Driven

MAN 20.280 BFAEG

Military vehicles have long fig-ured prominently in MAN's truck business. The 6 by 6 vehicle in the picture is derived from a military chassis and, with its combination of six-wheeled trac-tion and high power, has done well in successive Paris-Dakar rallies. The engine in the 20.280 incorporates MAN's M-type combustion chamber which is noted for its smooth, quiet run-ning.

Engine: MAN 11.4 litre, 6-cylinder turbocharged diesel, 280bhp.
Gvw: Up to 20 tonnes.

Astra

In 1946 Astra began by recon-ditioning Second World War army trucks, before starting in 1954 to build mainly off-road dumptrucks.

Engine: Detroit Diesel two-stroke, various power option.
Gearbox: Allison fully automatic.
Gvw: 30 tonnes.

Ural 4320

Primitive by Western standards, the 6 by 6 Ural nevertheless serves its purpose – to haul agricultural produce from collec-tive farms with or without a trailer.

Engine: KAMAZ 10.8 litre, V8 diesel, 210bhp.
Gearbox: 5-speed constant mesh.

Rigid, 4 Axles, 2 Driven

Engine: Cummins 10 litre, Gardner 10.4 litre or Perkins 12.2 litre, 6-cylinder turbo diesels.
Gearbox: Fuller 9-speed constant mesh.

ERF E-series

Britain's last independent truck builder updated its entire range in 1986. The most notable feature of the 8 by 4 E10 and E12 models is the spacious and comfortable cab. The cab shell is unique in Europe because it is moulded from hot-pressed glass-reinforced plastic which gives great strength and a smooth outer finish.

Foden S108

Since 1980 Foden has been part of the American Paccar group. The company's engineering now follows US practice, with the customer able to choose from a wide range of components.

Engine: Cummins, Caterpillar Gardner or Perkins 6-cylinder turbo diesels.
Gearbox: Fuller 9-speed or Spicer 10-speed contant mesh.

Mercedes-Benz 3025K D

Launched in 1985 this model fills a gap in Mercedes' otherwise comprehensive chassis range.

Engine: Mercedes 14.6 litre V8 diesel.
Gearbox: Mercedes 7-speed or ZF 16-speed.

Leyland Constructor-8 GB

The Constructor-8 is successor to the Scammell Routeman, whose chassis it retains.

Engine: Cummins, Leyland or Perkins 6-cylinder turbocharged diesels.
Gearbox: Spicer 10-speed.

Volvo FL10 S

Volvo's eight-wheelers are assembled at the company's Irvine plant in Scotland, although most of the parts are shipped from Sweden. There is also a smaller, less powerful model known as the FL7, which was the successor to the popular F7. Both FL models have a completely new cab which sits low on the chassis and features an American-style wrap-around fascia.

Engine: Volvo 9.6 litre, 6-cylinder turbo-intercooled diesel, 291bhp.
Gearbox: 8-speed synchromesh.

MAN 30.281 VFAK

Rigid vehicles with four axles have become more popular in countries like West Germany and the Netherlands following local legislation changes. For use in poor site conditions an 8 by 8 variant is offered.

Engine: MAN 11.4 litre, 6-cylinder turbocharged diesel, 280bhp (206kW).
Gearbox: Fuller 13-speed constant mesh.
Gvw: 34 tonnes.

Oshkosh (USA)

Since 1917 when the company was founded Oshkosh has specialised in building all-wheel drive heavy trucks for use off the road and in difficult winter conditions. This mixer is something of an Oshkosh speciality: the load is discharged at the front and the engine driving the mixer drum and the chassis is mounted at the back.

Engine: To customer's choice, notably Detroit Diesel and Caterpillar.
Gearbox: Allison automatic or Fuller manual.
Gvw: tonnes.

Rigid, 5 Axles, 4 Driven

Terberg F3000 (NL)

Though a Dutch company Terberg has in recent years worked closely with Volvo from Sweden, using Volvo cabs and engines in particular. Its trucks serve a market in which Volvo does not compete. The 10 by 8 shown, which can haul a total weight of over 50 tonnes, is typical.

Engine: Volvo 12 litre, 6-cylinder turbocharged diesel, 320bhp.
Gearbox: Fuller 13-speed constant mesh.

Articulated, 2 Axles, 1 Driven

Bedford TM3800 (GB)

In 1974 General Motors' UK truck-building subsidiary launched the new TM range, which included middleweight trucks and some diesel-powered heavies. The TM3800 is the heaviest 4 by 2 tractor, now manufactured with Cummins engines. Bedford had only limited success with the TM because they were competing against companies with more experience in the heavy vehicle field. In 1986 the company announced plans to withdraw from the market all weight categories above 35 tonnes gvw.

Engine: Cummins 10 or 14 litre, 6-cylinder turbocharged diesel, 290bhp.
Gearbox: Fuller 9-speed or Spicer 10-speed constant mesh.
Gvw: 38 tonnes.

Engine: Hino 13.3 litre, 6-cylinder or 16.7 litre V8 diesel, 260bhp or 320bhp.
Gearbox: 6/9-speed synchromesh.
Gvw: 38 tonnes.

Hino SH (J)

Japanese heavy trucks lagged behind their European counterparts both stylistically and technically for many years. The new Hino SH models, launched in 1982, were intended to change this situation. A safe and more comfortable cab was designed, and more efficient engine and new gearbox incorporated.

Engine: Pegaso 11.9 litre, 6-cylinder turbo diesel, 310bhp.
Gearbox: ZF 16-speed synchromesh or Fuller 9-speed constant mesh.
Gvw: 38 tonnes.

Pegaso 1231T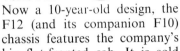

By European standards, Pegaso chassis from the Spanish state-owned Enasa group are now rather dated. But as a result of collaboration with DAF of the Netherlands, a new cab will be produced in 1987, which will update the image of the marque. Spain's entry to the EEC is expected to widen Pegaso's markets, which in turn is likely to prompt a move to give future designs a more international appeal.

Volvo F12

Now a 10-year-old design, the F12 (and its companion F10) chassis features the company's big flat-fronted cab. It is sold with an elaborately equipped sleeper known as the Globetrotter, for international haulage.

Engine: Volvo 12 litre, 6-cylinder turbo-intercooled diesel, 385bhp.
Gearbox: Volvo 12-speed synchromesh.
Gvw: 44 tonnes.

Articulated, 3 Axles, 1 Driven

ERF E-series  GB

Legislation in Britain was revised in 1983, allowing articulated trucks to carry higher total weights. Three-axled tractors like the ERF with an extra air-suspended centre axle became very popular. The latest E-series models have spacious and well-appointed cabs. ERF usually uses Cummins engines and Fuller gearboxes in a move to standardize production and to reduce costs. Variations are available, for example Gardner and Perkins Eagle diesels, but only at extra cost.

Engine: Cummins 10/14 litre, 6-cylinder turbo-intercooled diesels, 290 or 320bhp
Gearbox: Fuller 9-speed constant mesh.
Gvw: 38 tonnes.

MAN 22.321 **D**

Since the mid '60s, legislation in West Germany has encouraged the use of light 6 by 2 articulated trucks. MAN's chassis for this market are long-established, with air suspension standard on the two rearmost axles. Two wheelbases and three engine powers (280, 320 and 360bhp) are listed. All 6 by 2 chassis are powered by a large capacity, 12 litre engine. In 1986 a more modern and aerodynamic cab was introduced (*see picture*) called the F90 which will gradually replace the older design.

Engine: MAN 12 litre, 6-cylinder engine, 320bhp.
Gearbox: ZF 16-speed synchromesh or Fuller 13-speed constant mesh.
Gvw: 38 tonnes.

Articulated, 3 Axles, 2 Driven

Engine: Ashok-Leyland 11.1 litre, 6-cylinder diesel.
Gearbox: 5-speed constant mesh.

Ashok-Leyland Hippo (IND)

For over 30 years Ashok has built medium and heavy truck chassis, based on what are now rather dated British Leyland models. The 6 by 4 Hippo is one of a range of two- and three-axled chassis catering for com-bination weights up to 26 tonnes. Other models include the Taurus and Tusker. Cabs are built locally using flat, easily-repaired panels. Engines and gearboxes are made under licence from Leyland.

Engine: Caterpillar, Detroit Diesel or Cummins diesel (to customer's choice), up to 450bhp.
Gearbox: Fuller 15-speed constant mesh.
Gvw: 37.2 tonnes.

Ford LTL-9000 (USA)

When the overall length of a truck is limited a manufacturer cannot afford to waste potential load space, and so a bonneted layout is unsuitable. But relaxation of length limits for trucks in the US has revived interest in bonneted (or 'conventional') designs for both articulated and double-bottom drawbar combinations. The LTL models from Ford's Louisville range date from 1981, and are among the most modern conventionals.

GMC Astro 95

General Motors, like its main rival, Ford, offers a choice of forward-control ('cab–over') and bonneted ('conventional') heavy trucks. The Astro is GMC's most popular cab-over model. For its design more attention has been paid to aerodynamics than in any previous GMC model. The main cab has been tested in a wind tunnel and has been contoured for minimum drag. A cab roof deflector can also be specified to direct airflow over and round the trailer, minimizing turbulence in the gap behind the cab. As an indication of the extent to which US manufacturers are prepared to meet individual buyer's whims, the latest GMC 'cab-over' tractors are listed in nearly 100 different cab colour schemes, and very luxurious trims can be specified.

Engine: Detroit Diesel, Caterpillar or Cummins diesel (to customer's choice), up to 450bhp.
Gearbox: Fuller 9-speed constant mesh.
Gvw: 36.8 tonnes.

IH Eagle 9370 (USA)

Originally from the Navistar Corporation, the International Eagle 9370, launched in 1984, is from a range of 4 by 2 and 6 by 4 'conventional' chassis. They are easily identifiable by the new smoothly styled cab.

Engine: Choice of 10 from Cummins, Detroit Diesel and Caterpillar diesels, up to 475bhp.
Gearboxes: choice of 9 (constant mesh) from Fuller and Spicer.
Gvw: Up to 54 tonnes.

Engine: Cummins 14 litre, 6-cylinder turbocharged diesel, 300bhp, with numerous options.
Gearbox: Fuller 13-speed constant mesh.
Gvw: 45 tonnes.

Kenworth T600A (USA)

The T600A breaks with Paccar group tradition, not least in its aerodynamic styling. Unlike all the other trucks on this page, fuel tank, air cleaner and batteries are hidden. As a result fuel efficiency is said to benefit by over twenty per cent. Through its UK subsidiary, Foden, Paccar has had the opportunity to study European truck design more closely than many of its main American rivals.

Engine: Cummins 14 litre, 6-cylinder turbo-intercooled diesel, 400bhp.
Gearbox: Fuller 13-speed constant mesh.

Marmon 86-P (USA)

Marmon is one of the lesser-known American truck marques. Manufactured at Garland in Texas, Marmon is like many other US truck companies in that it offers the customer a choice of engines and transmissions, with Cummins 300 (turbocharged) and 400 (turbo-intercooled) bhp units as favourites. The Marmon tends to be favoured by those drivers who own their truck, and who want to be able to stamp their own individuality on the vehicle.

Mack Ultraliner (USA)

In its MH-603 form the Ultraliner is a 'cab-over' articulated truck. It is available with a sleeper cab with air suspension. Mack's own Econodyne engine is the usual power unit though Cummins and Detroit Diesels are listed options.

Engine: Mack 11 litre, 6-cylinder turbocharged diesel, 300bhp.
Gearbox: Mack 5-speed synchromesh.

Peterbilt 362

Design of American 'cab-over' heavy trucks has changed even less than that of 'conventionals'. The Paccar group's Peterbilt 362 exemplifies this conservative approach, with its coachbuilt non-aerodynamic cab styling, which has remained unchanged in almost 30 years.

Engine: Caterpillar 18 litre V8 turbocharged diesel, 450bhp.
Gearbox: Fuller 13-speed constant mesh.

164

Engine: Cummins 10/14 litre, 290 to 400bhp, Perkins 12.2 litre or Caterpillar 10.5/14.6 litre.
Gearbox: Fuller 9/13-speed or Fuller 10-speed.
Gvw: 38 tonnes.

Foden S106T

Unlike most UK heavy truck builders Foden (now owned by Paccar of the US) has specialized in 6 by 4 tractors for 38 tonne articulated combinations. Nearly all rivals offer 6 by 2 only. The traction given by the extra two driven wheels allow this truck to be used on poor ground, for tipping and for haulage. Despite its power the S106T is light, thanks to its aluminium chassis and high-tensile mainrails.

Scammell S24

Similar in many respects to the Landtrain built by parent company Leyland (*see page 149*), the bonneted Scammel S24 is however intended for very heavy-haulage duties.

Engine: Cummins 14 litre, 6-cylinder turbo-intercooled diesel, 350bhp.
Gearbox: Fuller 15-speed constant mesh or Allison automatic.
Gvw: Up to 150 tonnes.

Autocar USA

Autocar concentrates on building a low number of trucks which are tailored to individual buyers' requirements. The 6 by 4 bonneted ('conventional') tractors include some of the most old-fashioned looking trucks built anywhere in the world. They are however acknowledged for their extreme ruggedness and long life, facts which help Autocar to sell its chassis in many Third World territories. Their simple construction also makes servicing and repairs easy, an important consideration when trucks are operating in primitive conditions, far from a well-equipped workshop. Flat cab panels can be readily replaced from whatever materials are available locally, as can the window glass and simple chassis components.

Engine and gearbox: To customer's choice with Caterpillar 18 litre V8 diesel as most powerful option, 450bhp

Gvw: Up to 60 tonnes.

Specialist Trucks

Shelvoke Roadchief

The British Shelvoke Dempster company is one of the few refuse collector builders to manufacture its own chassis – the low quantities needed usually make it uneconomic. The Shelvoke Roadchief uses a glass-fibre crew cab with wide entry steps, for easy access.

Engine: Leyland 5.6 litre or Perkins 5.8 litre, 6-cylinder turbocharged diesel engine, 155bhp.
Gearbox: 5-speed constant or synchromesh.
Gvw: 16.26 tonnes.

EWK Bison

Though originally a military truck the Bison became available to civilian buyers in 1980. It stays afloat with the aid of massive inflatable rubber bags at each side which, when not in use, stow in two lockers underneath the truck.

Engine: Deutz 12 litre V8 air-cooled turbocharged diesel, 320bhp.
Gearbox: ZF automatic, switchable to twin steering propellers.
Gvw: 11 tonnes.

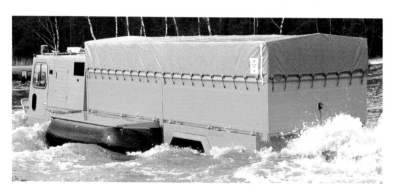

Iveco 6640G

Nicknamed the 'Jacare' (Portuguese for alligator) because of its mobility on land and water, the 6640G vehicle can carry 14 people plus a crew of two. It was built for a Cousteau Society expedition to the Amazon basin. Though shaped like a boat it can travel overland at up to 100km/h (60mph), independent suspension giving a smooth ride. Because of its novelty value the Jacare has been used for publicity purposes around the world, helping to make the name of Fiat's truck-building subsidiary better-known.

Engine: Fiat 5.5 litre, 6-cylinder diesel, 195bhp
Gearbox: 3-speed automatic. Multi-directional hydrojets for water propulsion.

Engine: Detroit Diesel V8 two-stroke diesel.
Gearbox: Clark power-shift.
Gvw: 26 tonnes.

Terra Flex TF300TT 〔CAN〕

All-terrain vehicles have been built by Terra Flex at Calgary, Alberta for over 30 years. They are used by the gas and oil explo- ration industry. The TF300TT has large-diameter deep-tread flotation tyres, which make it easy to travel over soft ground.

Foremost Commander C 〔CAN〕

Like the Terra Flex truck shown above, and built in the same Canadian town, the 6 by 6 Fore- most Commander is primarily a rugged oilfield vehicle able to negotiate exceptionally soft ground. An 8 by 8 version is also produced, for carrying loads of up to 40 tonnes.

Engine: Detroit Diesel 9.3 litre, V8 two-stroke diesel, 350bhp.
Gearbox: Clark power shift.
Gvw: 56.8 tonnes.

Dumptrucks

Euclid R-85 (USA)

Under various ownerships, currently the Clark Corporation, Euclid has built off-road dumptrucks since 1934. The R-85 machine, though medium-sized by Euclid standards, can nevertheless carry 77 tonnes of payload. Heavier machines in the Euclid range can carry loads of up to 154 tonnes. They make use of a novel form of electric drive, with motors in the wheel-hubs. The engine on these models drives a generator which supplies a current to the hub motors. This system provides excellent traction, especially when starting from a standstill. The R-85 however has a more conventional engine and transmission.

Engine: Cummins 38 litre, V12 turbo-intercooled diesel, 800bhp
Gearbox: Allison 6-speed automatic.
Gvw: 128.3 tonnes.

Caterpillar 773B USA

'Cat' is the biggest and probably the world's best known manufacturer of earth-moving equipment. The 773B dumptruck, which has a nominal capacity of 50 tonnes, is in the middle of the Caterpillar dumptruck weight range, which extends up to vehicles with the capacity to carry 150 tonnes.

Engine: Caterpillar 27 litre, V12 turbocharged diesel, 650bhp.
Gearbox: Cat automatic.
Gvw: 83.3 tonnes.

Aveling Barford RD255 GB

Through the 1970s – and until 1983 – A-B was owned by British Leyland, now it is run by a private investment group. The RD255, the company's heaviest dumptruck is at the top end of the Centaur range. Its notable features include nitrogen-oil telescopic suspension and automatic transmission.

Engine: Cummins 18.9 litre, 6-cylinder turbo-intercooled diesel.
Gearbox: Allison Torqmatic.
Gvw: 85.3 tonnes.

Engine: Detroit Diesel 14 litre, V12 two-stroke, 456bhp
Gearbox: Allison 6-speed automatic.

Astra BM35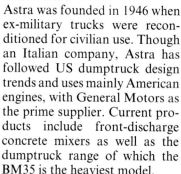

Astra was founded in 1946 when ex-military trucks were reconditioned for civilian use. Though an Italian company, Astra has followed US dumptruck design trends and uses mainly American engines, with General Motors as the prime supplier. Current products include front-discharge concrete mixers as well as the dumptruck range of which the BM35 is the heaviest model.

Belaz 7521 SU

The Russian Belaz can carry up to 180 tonnes of rock or opencast coal. It is produced in two versions, one of which uses a railway locomotive engine and transmission with a slow-revving engine. In both cases power is fed to 560kW electric motors in the wheel hubs.

Engine: 87.3 litre V12 turbocharged diesel, 2300bhp.
Gearbox: None (electric drive to hub motors).

Panel Vans

Engine: 1.6/2 litre petrol or 2.5 litre direct-injection diesel, 63/77/68bhp.
Gearbox: 5-speed synchromesh.
Gvw: Up to 3.5 tonnes.

Ford Transit

After 20 years in production with only minor external changes, the Transit range was redesigned in 1985. It is still rear-wheel drive, but the new wedge-fronted body cuts down on fuel consumption, and provides a more comfortable and better designed cab.

Renault Master

With the lighter traffic, the Master competes directly against the Transit. It has the unusual feature of both front and rear drive.

Engine: 2 litre petrol or 2.4 litre diesel, 80/74bhp.
Gearbox: 5-speed synchromesh.
Gvw: 3.5 tonnes.

VW Transporter

Volkswagen's rear-engine rear-drive vans were derived 30 years ago from the Beetle car. Major updates include a switch to water-cooled engines.

Engine: 2 litre petrol or 1.6 litre diesel, 60/50/70 (turbo) bhp.
Gearbox: 4/5-speed synchromesh.
Gvw: 2.46 tonnes.

Engine: 1.5 litre petrol, 68bhp.
Gearbox: 4-speed synchromesh.
Gvw: 1.98 tonnes.

Toyota Lite-ace

Toyota is Japan's largest vehicle maker, and second largest in the world. It builds a range of 'commercials' including the popular Hi-Lux, which can carry a payload of one tonne, and the Hi-ace. The newer, Lite-ace can carry loads up to about 800kg. It competes directly with the Nissan Vanette *(shown above)*.

Talbot Express

This range of 'commercials' is sold under four different marque names, (Talbot, Fiat, Peugeot and Citroën) and both front-wheel drive vans and chassis-cabs were introduced in 1983. They are the result of a joint Peugeot-Fiat group project. Engine options vary from model to model.

Engine: 1.8/2 litre petrol or 2.5 litre diesel, 69/78/75bhp.
Gearbox: 4/5-speed synchromesh.
Gvw: Up to 3.5 tonnes.

Engine: 1.7/2 litre petrol and 2/2.5 litre diesel, 72/92/61/73bhp.
Gearbox: 5-speed synchromesh.
Gvw: Up to 3.5 tonnes.

Freight Rover Sherpa **GB**

The Sherpa van's design can be traced back to the J4 models built by BMC in the 1960s. The Sherpa appeared in 1977, and its bonneted layout allows much easier access to the cab. A wider and heavier version, aimed at the same market as the 3.5 tonne Ford Transit, was launched in 1983. The latest diesel versions are powered by Perkins' new 2 litre Prima engine – the world's smallest direct-injection unit.

Mercedes-Benz T1 **D**

Dating from 1977, the T1 range are Mercedes' lightest commercials, and sell mainly in diesel form as expensive but durable delivery vehicles. The highly-regarded 2.4 litre Mercedes diesel is now rather dated in design, and does not have either fuel injection or turbocharging.

Engine: 2.3 litre petrol or 2.4 litre diesel, 94/71bhp.
Gearbox: 5-speed synchromesh.
Gvw: Up to 4.6 tonnes.

Glossary

All-wheel drive A vehicle which has all its road wheels powered. In the case of cars, also referred to as 4WD or 4 × 4.

Alternator An engine-driven unit which provides electric power and charges the battery. More efficient than the older dynamo system.

Articulated Short form 'artic'. A truck with tractor unit and separate semi-trailer joined by fifth wheel coupling (qv), allowing the two parts to 'hinge' while cornering.

Benzine An early form of fuel for cars, of similar constitution to the petrol and gasoline used now.

Big end The bottom part of the connecting rod that joins the crankshaft (qv) to the piston (qv).

BHP Initials standing for Brake Horse Power, indicating the power output of an engine. Originally based on the work done by one horse, it is now measured more scientifically. Sometimes expressed in kilowatt units (1 hp = 0.745 kW) American bhp figures are usually higher and are based on a different calculation.

Bodyshell The complete body of a modern car before the components are attached and installed.

Bonnetted The layout of a truck in which the driver sits behind the engine, as in a passenger car. In the USA, called 'conventional'.

Camshaft Part of an engine, responsible for controlling the opening and closing of the valves. The rotating shaft has specially-designed asymmetrical bumps on it that trigger levers to push down or lift off the valve stem.

Carburettor An instrument which controls the mixture of air and fuel to be drawn into the engine for combustion.

Chassis The frame upon which the wheels, suspension components and the engine/gearbox/driveline are fixed. Early cars had a separate chassis, modern cars use a monococque (qv) construction.

Clutch The means by which the engine, gearbox and transmission are connected and disconnected. Usually done by means of a special plate, covered in friction material and moved backwards and forwards by a pedal linkage.

Crankshaft The big shaft in the bottom of the engine to which the pistons are attached. Its shape and construction convert the up-and-down piston movement into a rotary motion to drive the wheels.

Cut-in The way in which the rear wheels of a truck or its trailer follow a line *inside* that of the front wheels when the rig is cornering.

CVT Initials standing for Continuously Variable Transmission – a system of belts and pulleys which replaces conventional gearboxes and does away with gearchanging. The vehicle is always in the right gear.

Cylinder The part of the engine in which the controlled explosion of fuel and air takes place to provide the power.

Dampers Also known as shockabsorbers, they act to smooth out the up-and-down motion of the suspension created as the wheels ride over bumps.

Day cab A short cab on a truck of lorry, without built-in sleeping accommodation.

Diesel A special type of engine, very commonly used on trucks. The main difference between diesel and petrol engines is that the diesel has no sparking plugs.

Direct injection A fuel injection system for diesel engines in which the fuel is squirted directly into the combustion chamber, instead of a small pre-chamber as in conventional diesels.

Differential A gear system operating on the driven axle that allows for the difference in travel distance between the inside and outside wheels when cornering, so preventing the risk of one wheel locking up and skidding (*see diagram*).

▼ **Differential:** when a car is cornering the outer wheels travel further than the inner wheels. The differential unit allows the outer wheels to turn faster.

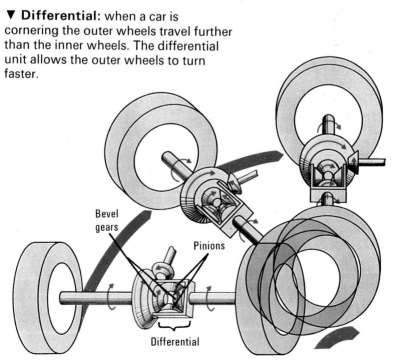

Bevel gears

Pinions

Differential

Disc brakes A very powerful braking system, developed in motor racing. The wheel is stopped by a pair of callipers pressing pads of friction material on to each side of a steel disc, attached to the wheel hub.

Distributor An electrical device to distribute a high tension current to the spark plugs at the right time to fire the fuel/air mixture in the cylinder and combustion chamber. More cars are using electronic systems, making the distributor redundant.

▲ A 'forward control' or 'cab-over' truck.

Double bottom An articulated truck towing a drawbar trailer to form an extra-long vehicle. Common in some American states.

Drawbar trailer A trailer supported wholly on its own wheels, and hitched to a truck by a towbar.

Emission control Many governments now demand very high standards for 'clean' exhausts, including a phasing out or ban on the use of fuel containing poisonous additives such as lead.

Fifth wheel coupling A device for connecting the two sections of an articulated truck so that the rig can 'bend' at the join, and so that the tractor can easily be detached from the semi-trailer.

Forward control The truck layout in which the driver sits alongside the engine, with no bonnet sticking out ahead of the windscreen. Called 'cab-over' in the USA.

Fuel injection An advance on the carburettor (qv), in that the f.i. system injects a measured quantity of fuel *directly* into the combustion chamber instead of making the engine draw the mixture in along pipes.

FWD Abbreviation for Front Wheel Drive, an increasingly common arrangement for small and medium-sized cars, usually with the engine positioned crossways at the front to allow more passenger space.

Gross weight The weight of a truck complete with its load. Usually abbreviated to GVW (Gross Vehicle Weight) or, in the case of articulated vehicles, GCW (Gross Combination Weight). The weight of a truck *without* its load is Tare weight.

Gudgeon pin A metal pin used to join the piston to the connecting rod through the little end (qv).

Halogen The gas used to make headlamp systems. An envelope of quartz carries inside it a tungsten filament that glows when electricity passes through and heats it. Halogen gas inside makes it produce a stronger light.

Hydrolastic A clever new car suspension system developed for the Morris 1100 which uses water-filled rubber springs. A later development used gas (hydragas).

ICE Short form for In-Car-Entertainment, covering radios, tape players and compact disc machines as well as television (for back seat passengers only!).

Intercooler A device used with turbocharging that cools down the air after it leaves the turbo (qv) but before it enters the combustion chamber. Cooler, more dense air aids the combustion process.

Landing gear Legs that can be wound down to support the front of a semi-trailer after it has been uncoupled from the tractor unit.

Monocoque Used to describe the body of a car which does not have a separate chassis (qv), in other words it is made all in one piece.

Overdrive Before five-speed gearboxes became common on cars, manufacturers used to fit special overdrive units – in effect a kind of auxiliary gearbox – that could be switched in and out electrically to provide extra, higher gears when needed.

Piston The piston fits tightly into the cylinder of an engine and does the job of sucking in the fuel/air mixture and blowing out the exhaust, as well as being pushed down by the ignited mixture in order to provide the power stroke.

Payload The weight of the load a truck can carry.

Powertrain The engine, gearbox and axles on a car or truck.

Rack and pinion A form of steering system using a toothed plate fixed to the rods joining the wheels, and a gear pinion worked by the steering wheel that moves it from side to side, turning the wheels.

RPM The short form for revolutions per minute, usually of an engine, indicated on the tachometer in the instrument panel.

▼ **The latest Volvo truck** diesel engine showing the intercooler in front of the main radiator.

Servo Usually found as an addition to a braking system, the servo simply allows the effort of the driver's foot on the pedal to be magnified.

Semi-trailer A trailer supported at the rear on its own axle and at the front on the chassis of a matching tractor unit.

Supercharger The supercharger does a similar job to the turbocharger (qv) except that it is driven by belts or chains from the engine. Like the turbo, it effectively force feeds the engine with air.

Synchromesh The device in a gearbox that allows gears to be changed without crunching, helping to overcome the problem of matching the speeds of the engine and gearbox.

Tachograph A special instrument in the cab of a truck that records the progress of the truck on the road, such as speeds, rest times etc. An unpopular device with many drivers.

Torque Used to describe the rotating or twisting force of an engine. The best gauge of an engine's torque output is obtained by assessing the way in which it pulls up hills, without having to change gear.

Turbocharger Similar to the supercharger (qv) except that it has a compressor turbine driven by the exhaust gases of the engine.

6×4, 4×2 etc A convenient means of indicating the number of wheels on a truck (first figure) and how many are driven (second figure). In Europe a twin-tyred wheel counts as one wheel, in the USA as two wheels.

Useful Books

The New Observer's Book of Automobiles by Stuart Bladon (Warne, 1986)

Complete Encyclopaedia of Motorcars 1888 to the Present ed. N. Georgano (Ebury Press, 1982)

The New Observer's Book of Trucks (Warne, 1986)

World Truck Handbook ed. N. Georgano (Jane's, 1986)

Anatomy of the Motor Car ed. Ian Ward (Orbis, 1985)

The Centenary Encyclopaedia of Automobiles (Newnes, 1984)

The Centenary of the Car (Octopus Books, 1984)

One Hundred Years of the Motor Car 1886 to 1986 ed. Ruiz (Collins, 1985)

Magazines

Cars (United Kingdom)
W = Weekly   M = Monthly
Autocar (W), *Autosport* (W), *Car* (M), *Classic Car* (M), *Classic and Sports Car* (M), *Fast Lane* (M), *Motor Sport* (M), *Performance Car* (M)

Cars (United States)
Automobile (M), *Autoweek* (W), *Car and Driver* (M), *Motor Trend* (M), *Road and Truck* (M)

Commercials (United Kingdom)
Commercial Motor (W), *Motor Transport* (W), *Truck* (M)

Museums

United Kingdom and the Continent

National Motor Museum, Beaulieu, Hampshire (Cars and commercials some of them available to ride)
Stratford Motor Museum, Stratford-upon-Avon (Cars)
Midland Motor Museum, Coventry (Cars)
British Museum of Road Transport, Coventry (Cars and trucks)
The Donnington Collection, Donnington Park (Single-seater racing cars)
British Motor Industry Heritage Collection, Syon Park, Middlesex (Large collection of British cars)
Schlumpf Collection, Mulhouse, France (Vast private collection, including many rare Bugattis)
Dutch National Motor Museum, Raamsdonkerveer near Breda, Netherlands
Autoworld, Mahy, Brussels, Belgium
Biscaretti Collection, Turin, Italy
BMW History Museum, Munich, Germany
Also worth looking at **The Science Museum,** Kensington, London

▶ **A Bugatti** in the Ford Museum, Detroit.

◀ **A 1959 Argonaut** Motor Machine from the Blackhawk Collection.

United States

Ford Museum, Greenfield Village, Detroit, Michigan (General transport museum)
Harrah Motor Museum, Reno, Nevada (Unfortunately now almost dismantled)

General Information

The Society of Motor Manufacturers and Traders, Forbes House, Halkin Street, London
Road Haulage Association, 104 New King's Road, London
Historic Commercial Vehicle Society, Iden Garage, Staplehurst, Kent
Freight Transport Association, Hermes House, St John's Road, Tunbridge Wells, Kent

Index

Acknowledgements

A.B. International 171 bottom; Acorn Studios 117 top; American Motors Corp 79 top; Asatsu 135 bottom; Ashok Leyland Ltd 160 top; Astra 172 top; Audi AG 103 top; Austin Rover Group Ltd 70 top, 72 bottom, 112 top; Autocar 11; Autosport 42; AVTO Export 151 bottom right; Bedford Commercial Vehicles 147 bottom; 156 top; Tim Blakemore 134 top, 136, 141 top, 148 top, 150 top, 151 top & bottom left, 153 top left, 159 bottom, 162 bottom, 165 top, 174, 175 bottom; B.M.W. 45, 48, 56 top, 104 top; Bombardier Inc 169 top; Bosch 51, 52; Sam Brown 55, 75 bottom, 76 top, 78 bottom, 88 bottom, 91 top, 96 bottom, 99, 100 top, 113; Alan Bunting 128, 130, 144 bottom; Caterham Car Sales & Coachworks Ltd 56 bottom; Caterpillar Overseas SA 171 top; Chrysler Corp 67 top; Chrysler/Plymouth P.R. 75 top, 89 bottom; Citroen 36, 93 top, 102 top, 112 bottom; Citroen U.K. 82 bottom left; Classic & Sports Car 14, 34, 37, 38, 49; Colt Car Co 79 bottom, 109 bottom; Commercial Motor 132; DAF Trucks 134 bottom; Daimler-Benz 145 bottom; De Tomaso SpA 60 bottom; Dennis Eagle 135 top; Dodge Trucks 76 bottom; ERF Ltd 138 bottom, 152 top; E.W.K. 167 bottom; Excalibur Automobile Corp 64 top; Fiat 96 top, 118 top, 125 bottom; First Automobile Works 91 bottom; Foden Trucks 152 bottom; Ford Motor Co Ltd 30 bottom, 69 top, 72 top, 83 bottom, 139 top, 173 top; Ford U.S.A. 65, 108 top, 140 top; F.S.O. 118 bottom; Fuji Heavy Industries 110; G.G.K. London Ltd 98 top; General Motors 31 top, 63, 108 bottom; Buick Div., General Motors 89 top; Ginaf Trucks 146 top; Robert Harding Picture Library 122, 127 top; Haymarket Publishing 8, 19, 23, 24, 26, 30 top, 33, 40, 124, 181; Hino Motors Ltd 138 top, 144 bottom, 156 bottom; Holden 101 bottom; Hyundai Motor Co 120; Isuzu Motors Ltd 109 top, 141 top right; Ital Design 44 top; Iveco Ford Truck Ltd 137 top; Jaguar Cars Ltd 58 top; Kenworth Truck Co 148 bottom; Lamborghini 62 top; John Lamm 111 top; Lancia 94 bottom, 98 bottom; Land Rover Group 77 bottom, 78 top, 175 top; Leyland Vehicles 133, 153 top right; Lincoln-Mercury Div. 88 top, 90 top; Lotus Cars Ltd 58 bottom; Mack Trucks Inc 126, 163 top, 178; Marmon Truck Co 163 bottom; Maserati UK Ltd 62 bottom; Mazda Cars UK Ltd 22, 39, 64 bottom, 71 top; John McGovern 16, 182; Mercedes Benz 29, 32, 77 top; Morgan Motor Co Ltd 59 top; Navistar International Corp 162 top; Nissan Motor Co Ltd 100 bottom; Novosti 140 bottom, 172 bottom; Adam Opel AG 70 bottom, 104 bottom, 115; Oshkosh Truck Corp 155 top; Oy Sisu-Auto AB 145 top; Panther Car Co Ltd 67 bottom; Pegaso Audio Visuals 141 bottom, 157 top; Peterbilt Motor Co 164; Peugeot 54; Pontiac 44 bottom, 53; Popperfoto 18 bottom, 41; Porsche Cars G.B. 43, 105 top; Jon Pressnell 125 top; Reliant Motors 59 bottom; Renault 15 bottom, 71 bottom, 82 bottom right, 137 bottom, 142 top, 173 bottom right; Rolls Royce Motors Ltd 31 bottom, 86, 87 top; Scammell Motors 165 bottom; Scania (G.B.) Ltd 146 bottom; Seddon Atkinson Vehicles Ltd 150 bottom; Shelvoke Dempster Ltd 167 top; Steyr 127 bottom; Stutz 90 bottom; Talbot Motor Co Ltd 27; Tatra 82 top; Terberg Benschop BV 155 bottom; Toyota Motor Corp 80, 101 top, 111 bottom, 121 bottom; TVR Engineering Ltd 60 top; Vauxhall-Opel Car Marketing 114 top; VAG U.K. Ltd 83 top, 173 bottom left; VEB Sachsenring 94 top; Volkswagenwerk AG 69 bottom, 114 bottom; Volvo Concessionaires Ltd 74, 105 bottom, 117 bottom, 131, 153 bottom, 157 bottom, 179; Volvo White Truck Corp 147 top; Wells Advertising 81 bottom, 121 top; ZEFA 28, 129.

Picture research: Jackie Cookson